Contents

KU-767-684

4 Reading

Introduction

This book contains:

- four complete Practice Tests for the Cambridge First Certificate in English (from December 2008)
- answer key, including mark schemes for all Writing tasks
- model answers for all Writing tasks
- guide to marking, including Do-it-yourself marksheets
- guidance on how to assess the Writing and Speaking papers
- sample answer sheets
- audio scripts

Exam content

Paper 1: Reading (1 hour 15 minutes)

	Text	Question type	Focus
PART 1	3 short texts linked to a general theme	4-option multiple-choice, 2 questions per text	comprehension of detail, opinion, attitude, purpose, main idea, specific information, implication, exemplification, reference, comparison, imagery, tone, style, etc. 6 questions; 12 marks
PART 2	1 text with 6 paragraphs missing	choice of 7 paragraphs to fill the gaps	understanding of text structure, links between parts of text 6 questions; 12 marks
PART 3	1 text (article, fiction, non-fiction)	4-option multiple choice	same as Part 1 7 questions; 14 marks
PART 4	1 text divided into sections OR several short texts	matching statements / information to section of text or short text they refer to or appear in	location of specific information / points; comprehension of paraphrasing 15 questions; 15 marks

Paper 2: Writing (1 hour 30 minutes)

	Task	Focus
PART 1	letter, article, report or proposal (180–220 words) Candidates **must** do this task.	evaluating, expressing opinions, hypothesizing, persuading 20 marks
PART 2	article, essay, report, review, proposal, letter, competition entry, or contribution to longer piece (e.g. guidebook or research project) (220–260 words) Questions 2–4: candidates choose one task from three choices OR Questions 5a / 5b: candidates may choose one task about the set books. (There are two set books and these change from time to time; therefore in this book, the set book tasks are generalized.)	varying according to the task, including comparing, giving advice, giving opinions, justifying, persuading 20 marks

with
key

CAE
Practice Tests

Four new tests for the revised CAE exam

MARK HARRISON

0

WITHDRAWN

OXFORD
UNIVERSITY PRESS

ACKNOWLEDGEMENTS

We would like to thank the following for permission to reproduce photographs: Alamy
pp31 (Corbis Super RF), 37c (Papilio), 37r (David Chapman), 53 (View Stock),
1302B (Homer Sykes), 1302C (Alex Segre), 131bl (Ron Niebrugge), 131br
(F.Bettex/Mysterra.org), 131c (Sylvia Cordaiy Photo Library Ltd), 131cr (Chad
Ehlers), 132bcr (Jenny Matthews), 132br (vario images GmbH & Co.KG),
132cl (The Photolibrary Wales), 132tc (eddie linssen), 132tl (LJSphotography),
133br (Janine Wiedel Photolibrary), 133cl (Janine Wiedel Photolibrary),
133tr (PhotoAlto), 1341A (Ingram Publishing/Superstock Limited), 1341C
(Frances Roberts), 1342B (Jeff Morgan education), 1342C (Wildscape), 135cl
(Lou Linwei), 135cr (photow.com), 137tl (Steve P.); Carol
Robertson p59; Corbis UK Ltd. pp51 (Heide Benser/zefa), 52 (Daniele La
Monaca/Reuters), 73 (Images.com), 132bl (Pierre Vauthey Sygma), 132c
(Rick Gomez), 1342A (Lucy Nicholson/Reuters), 1362A (Hunter/zefa), 1362C
(Burke/Triolo Productions/Brand); Fotolibra p37bl; Getty Images pp8 (Jeremy
Liebman), 9, 29 (Dorien Leigh/Mansell/Time Life Pictures), 37tl (Guy Edwardes/
The Image Bank), 1302A (Emmanuel Faure), 133bl (Justin Pumfrey), 135br
(Steve Allen), 1361A (Javier Pierini), 1361C (Thomas Hoeffgen), 1362B, 137
(Vote for Smith) (Digital Vision), 137tr (Menahem Kahana/AFP); iStockphoto
pp15 (Andrew Howe), 74 (Przemyslaw Rzeszutko); Martyn F. Chillmaid
p133cr; Oxford University Press pp75 (Photodisc), 1341B (Harry Sheridan),
135bl (Photodisc), 1361B (imagesource), 137 (magazines); Photofusion Picture
Library p133tl (Ulrike Preuss); Photolibrary Group pp131tl, 131tr, 135tl; Rex
Features pp1301C (ITV Archive), 132tcr (ITV Archive), 132tr; 137cl (Martin
Specht); Ronald Grant Archive pp32, 1301A, 1301B

*The authors and publisher are grateful to those who have given permission to reproduce
the following extracts and adaptations of copyright material:* p7 'The not so sweet
smell of success' by Roger Williams, Daily Telegraph, 02/04/05. © Telegraph
Media Group Limited, 2005; p8 'The sick building syndrome' by Amy
Iggulden, Daily Telegraph, 23/03/06. © Telegraph Media Group Limited, 2005;
p20 'Views of the departing staff are valuable' by Caroline Cook, Hendon and
Finchley Times, 23/03/06. Reproduced with permission. Extract courtesy of
Newsquest London Ltd; p23 'Unaccustomed as I am…' by Rosemary Behan,
Daily Telegraph, 25/11/06, © Telegraph Media Group Limited, 2006; p23
'Linking city with suburbia' by Janaki Mahadevan, Hendon and Finchley
Times, 02/11/06. Reproduced with permission. Extract courtesy of Newsquest
London Ltd; p24 'Tools of the trade' by Rachel Carlyle, Daily Telegraph,
11/09/04. © Telegraph Media Group Limited, 2004; p25 'Go on, snigger all you
like' by Rupert Christiansen, Daily Telegraph, 24/10/05. © Telegraph Media
Group Limited, 2005; p29 Adapted extracts from The Stone Diaries by Carol
Shields. Reproduced with permission. © Carol Shields 1994; p34 'Simply
ticking the boxes isn't enough' by DR James Rieley, Daily Telegraph, 31/03/05.
© Telegraph Media Group Limited, 2005; p37 'Winged winner and losers' by
Mark Cocker, Daily Telegraph Magazine, 20/08/05. © Telegraph Media Group
Limited, 2005; p41 'On track for a triple whammy' by Nicholas Roe, Daily
Telegraph, 17/06/06. © Telegraph Media Group Limited, 2006; p42'Who just
gets desserts?' The Press, 06/10/05. Reproduced with permission of The Barnet
Press; p47 'Novel in a year' by Louise Doughty, Daily Telegraph, 18/11/06.
© Telegraph Media Group Limited, 2006; p51 'Patience is almost a thing of
the past' by Sarah Womack, Daily Telegraph, 24/03/06. © Telegraph Media
Group Limited, 2006; p52 Extract from a novel Doctored evidence, by Donna
Leon, published by William Heinemann. Reprinted by permission of The
Random House Group Ltd; p56 Extract from a novel Brick Lane, by Monica
Ali, published by Doubleday. Reprinted by permission of The Random House
Group Ltd; p59 'The right stripes' by Frank Whitford, The Sunday Times,
04/09/05. © NI Syndication Ltd, 2005; p62 'The man who showed us the world'
by Eric Owen, Daily Telegraph, 04/02/06. © Telegraph Media Group Limited,
2006; p67 'Over 70 tried and tested great books to read aloud' by Jacqueline
Wilson. Excerpts from Simon Mayo show, Reproduced by kind permission
of BBC Radio 5; p67 'The Workout' by Sam Murphy, Hydro Active magazine
2006, © London Marathon Ltd, 2008; p69 'Invisible benefits' by Sian Griffiths,
The Sunday Times, 30/10/05. © NI Syndication, 2005; p73 'Trust your gut
instincts when those shopping decisions get tough, say scientists' by Roger
Highfield, Daily Telegraph, 17/02/06. © Telegraph Media Group Limited, 2006;
p75 'Success: it's a brain of two halves' by John Paul Flintoff and John Elliott,
The Sunday Times, 12/03/06. © NI Syndication Ltd, 2006; p84 'High notes of
the singing Neanderthals' by Jonathan Leake, The Sunday Times, 30/01/05.
© NI Syndication Ltd 2005; p85 'Discover the joys of reading' Hendon and
Finchley Times, 23/02/06. Reproduced with permission. Extract courtesy of
Newsquest London Ltd; p86 'Poles apart from just walking' by Caroline Cook,
Hendon and Finchley Times, July 06, Reproduced with permission. Extract
courtesy of Newsquest London Ltd.

*Although every effort has been made to trace and contact copyright holders before
publication, this has not been possible in some cases. We apologize for any apparent
infringement of copyright and if notified, the publisher will be pleased to rectify any errors
or omissions at the earliest opportunity.*

Paper 3: Use of English (1 hour)

	Text / Input	Question type	Focus
PART 1	1 short text with 12 gaps	4-option multiple-choice; choose the correct word(s) to fill each gap	vocabulary (meaning of single words, completion of phrases, phrasal verbs, etc.) 12 questions; 12 marks
PART 2	1 short text with 15 gaps	fill each gap with one word	mostly grammar, some vocabulary 15 questions; 15 marks
PART 3	1 short text with 10 gaps	use the words given to form the correct word for each gap	word formation 10 questions; 10 marks
PART 4	5 sets of three gapped sentences	fill the gaps with one word that is appropriate in all three sentences	vocabulary (meaning of single words, completion of phrases, phrasal verbs, etc.) 5 questions; 10 marks
PART 5	8 unrelated sentences, each followed by a single word and a gapped sentence	use the word given to complete the gapped sentence so that it means the same as the first sentence	grammar and vocabulary 8 questions; 16 marks *(1 mark for each part of the answer, max. 2 marks per question)*

Paper 4: Listening (40 minutes)

Each recording is heard twice. At the end of the exam, candidates are given 5 minutes to transfer their answers to the answer sheet.

	Recording	Question type	Focus
PART 1	3 short conversations	3-option multiple-choice (2 questions per piece)	detail, gist, opinion, feeling, attitude, function, purpose, agreement between speakers, course of action, topic, speaker / addressee, genre, place / situation 6 questions; 6 marks
PART 2	1 monologue	sentence completion: 8 sentences to complete with a word or short phrase	understanding of specific information given in the piece 8 questions; 8 marks
PART 3	1 interview or discussion (two or more speakers)	4-option multiple-choice	understanding of opinion, attitude, detail, gist 6 questions; 6 marks
PART 4	5 short monologues	matching: 2 tasks. For each task, match what each speaker says to 1 of 8 options	same as Part 1 10 questions; 10 marks

Paper 5: Speaking (15 minutes)

	Activity type (examiner + two candidates)	Focus
PART 1	conversation between candidates and examiner (3 mins)	general and personal topics relating to the candidate
PART 2	individual 'long turn' for each candidate with a brief response from second candidate (4 mins)	candidates talk about 2 sets of 3 pictures
PART 3	2-way conversation between candidates (4 mins)	candidates discuss a situation described in words and pictures in order to reach conclusions
PART 4	conversation between candidates and examiner (4 mins)	candidates discuss topics related to Part 3 task with the examiner 20 marks total

All papers have equal value: 20% of the total. For a guide to calculating marks, see page 100.

Paper 1: Reading (1 hour 15 minutes)

You are going to read three extracts which are all concerned in some way with buildings. For questions 1–6, choose the answer (A, B, C or D) which you think fits best according to the text.

Mark your answers on the separate answer sheet.

The not-so-sweet smell of Shakespeare's success

As you take your seat at the Globe Theatre on a summer's afternoon in 1600 for the premiere of Shakespeare's *Hamlet*, up to a thousand smelly
line 5 'groundlings' are jostling for standing room in the open-air courtyard at the front and sides of the stage, and 2,000 better-off (but not necessarily better-smelling) people may be crammed onto the narrow wooden benches of the three
line 11 vertically stacked galleries topped by a thatched roof. The performance begins at 2pm and runs without an interval. Audience participation is enthusiastic, with boos for the wicked Claudius, wails at Ophelia's death, and unpopular performances pelted with unsaleable vegetables. Performances are in broad daylight, so actors and audience are in
line 20 constant contact, and asides (scripted and ad lib) are frequent.

All performances are in contemporary dress, with costumes reflecting the character's social status rather than historical period. The poshest outfits may once have belonged to real noblemen – common people are forbidden by law to wear lordly attire, so aristocratic hand-me-downs often find their way into theatrical costume stores. There are props and furniture, and the wooden theatre is brightly painted, but there is no scenery, partly because, with the audience on three sides, many would be unable to see it. With fewer visual effects, the audience must use their imagination more than modern playgoers – helped by the visual
line 38 clues with which the dramatists pepper their work. Seeing the play is actually more important than hearing it. Many of the actors have not even had time to memorize their lines, but are reading them from paper rolls (hence our word 'role' for character).

1 Which of these words is used to illustrate audience behaviour at the theatre?

A jostling (line 5)
B stacked (line 11)
C asides (line 20)
D pepper (line 38)

[1]

2 Which aspect of theatrical performances in 1600 is emphasized in the text?

A the fact that they had some similarities with modern theatre
B the effort that went into making them entertaining
C the ways in which they reflected class divisions at the time
D the differences in the reactions of those involved in them

[2]

Sick building syndrome 'is result of poor management'

The workplace illness 'sick building syndrome', which is said to cost businesses millions of pounds each year, is caused by poor managers rather than a poor environment, a study says. Researchers found that the 10 symptoms commonly associated with the illness, which was identified by the World Health Organization more than 20 years ago, were linked to long hours and lack of support at work. The study found that workers in buildings with unacceptable levels of carbon dioxide, airborne fungi and noise were actually less likely to say that they were ill. It had been thought that poor air quality and airborne bacteria caused these symptoms.

Mai Stafford, the lead author on the study and a senior research fellow in epidemiology at University College London, said: 'We found no evidence that the buildings themselves are important in "sick building syndrome". It seems to be wrongly named. Psychological factors of work – stress brought on by lack of control, long hours and unsupportive managers – were far more important.' Alexi Marmot,

an architectural consultant who worked on the study, said the syndrome had been the result of 'overactive imaginations'.

Dr Stafford, reporting the findings in the British Medical Journal, said: 'The only area of the physical environment that had a significant effect on health was in control over the desk space. If employees could choose what lighting and heat they worked in, they were less likely to report symptoms. It shows that employers need to consider job stress above

an audit of physical properties.'

The findings could pose problems for the growing number of SBS consultants who will 'syndrome-proof' a building for about £1,000 a day. Richard Smith, a consultant whose work has included 'SBS-proofing' the Tower of London after fears were raised about photocopier fumes, said: 'Employers should still get their buildings looked at for SBS because then staff are going to feel more valued anyway – it will boost morale.'

3 One view of sick building syndrome expressed in the text is that

A managers do not take it seriously enough.

B it does not really exist.

C it is no longer a serious problem.

D the causes of it have changed.

| 3 |

4 The SBS consultant's opinion of the research is that

A the findings are not wholly correct.

B employers are unlikely to agree with the findings.

C his work is relevant to the findings.

D employees will welcome the findings.

| 4 |

The HEALING begins with HOSPITAL DESIGN

If there is one universal truth about hospitals, it is that they are drab, dismal places, not at all designed to heal. The furniture is hard-edged and bland. Lights are fluorescent and harsh. But architects around the world are working to humanize their design. The idea is: build inviting, soothing hospitals, with soft lighting, inspiring views, single rooms, curved corridors and relaxing gardens, and patients will heal quicker, nurses will remain loyal to their employers and doctors will perform better.

The idea of building hospitals that help rather than hinder recovery is beginning to gain support in Europe. Britain, which has some of the oldest, drabbest hospitals in Europe, is in the process of building 100 hospitals and is paying close attention to their design. A few European hospitals are being used as models for the rest of Europe, including the Norfolk and Norwich Hospital in England, the Groningen Academic Hospital in the Netherlands and, most notably, the Rikshospitalet University Hospital in Oslo, Norway.

'The environment in a hospital contributes to the therapy of the patients,' said Tony Monk, a British architect in health care design. 'People are mentally vulnerable when they come in, and if they are beaten down by an awful, dreadful, concrete, uninteresting, poor building with poor colors, it makes them even worse.'

Hoping to spread this philosophy as hospital construction is booming in the United States and Europe, the architects have new data to back their designs. Their research shows, for example, that patients who can see trees instead of cars from their windows recover more quickly.

5 The writer makes the assumption that
A patients notice hospital design more than experts think they do.
B hospital design used to be appropriate but no longer is.
C it is not difficult to improve hospital design.
D hospital design prevents hospitals from fulfilling their function.

[5]

6 The descriptive language used about hospitals in the text emphasizes
A how dark they are.
B how depressing they are.
C how varied they are.
D how important they are.

[6]

You are going to read a magazine article about a scientific expedition. Six paragraphs have been removed from the article. Choose from the paragraphs A–G the one which fits each gap (7–12). There is one extra paragraph which you do not need to use.

Mark your answers on the separate answer sheet.

So many species of fungi, so ripe for the discovery

In the Maya Mountains in Belize, Timothy J. Baroni stepped out of his tent and checked his gear: hunting knife, heavy boots, tackle box, sharp machete and two cigars. 'All set,' he said. 'Let's go find some fungi.' With that, Dr. Baroni and two colleagues, Dr. D. Jean Lodge and Dr. Dan Czederpiltz, plunged into the Central American jungle. The three are mycologists – mushroom experts – who spent ten days in August searching for new species in the mountains of southern Belize. The ridge they were exploring, Doyle's Delight, is 15 kilometers east of the Guatemalan border and was named for its resemblance to the prehistoric setting of Arthur Conan Doyle's novel *The Lost World*.

7

There were other researchers on the multinational expedition – a Belizean ornithologist, a British botanist, an American reptile specialist – but the mushroom experts have the best odds of finding a new species. Dr. David L. Hawksworth, the British mushroom expert, extrapolating from the ratio of fungi to vascular plants (six species of fungi for every plant) in several sets of data, has estimated the existence of 1.5 million species of fungi on earth.

8

Fungi are neither plants nor animals; they were only recognized as their own distinct kingdom in the 1970s. In 1983, research revealed that fungi are actually more closely related to animals than to plants. However, scientists can't agree on how many species of fungi have been identified – estimates range from 74,000 to 300,000.

9

The mushroom experts find new species by conscientiously following a workaday schedule, even in the jungle. Here, they spent mornings in the field collecting 20 to 30 specimens each day. In the afternoon they returned to their lab, a 3-meter by 3-meter screen tent, to process their specimens.

10

On the first morning at Doyle's Delight, Dr. Baroni didn't get 10 minutes down the trail before coming upon an intriguing specimen of bolete, a mushroom with pores instead of gills under its cap. He put his face up to the fungus, then pulled back to celebrate. 'That's outstanding. Yes!' he said, pumping his elbow like a champion golfer sinking a winning putt. 'That's worth the helicopter trip right there.'

11

A fungus, said Dr. Czederpiltz, a Forest Service mycologist based in Madison, Wisconsin, is 'just a mass of threadlike cells.' The part we see, the mushroom, is merely the fruiting body – like the apple on a tree. The body of the fungus is made up of those thread-like cells, known as mycelium, that are so small they can grow right through what we perceive as solid objects, like wood, leaves or toe-nails. Fungi are not, however, what you'd call a glamorous field of research.

12

Despite this lack of recognition, his enthusiasm is undimmed. 'This jungle is full of fungi,' he added as he crept slowly down a steep ridge. 'They're all around us.'

A   Each mushroom was then measured, precisely described, and noted for color. Then it was slowly baked for 24 hours in Dr. Lodge's field oven, a custom-made butane-powered drying rack.

B   'Only 5 to 10 per cent of those have been discovered and named,' said Dr. Baroni, a biology professor at the State University of New York at Cortland. (About 90 per cent of the world's 300,000 species of flowering plants have already been described.) Dr. Baroni, Dr. Lodge and two other mycologists not on this trip are in the final year of a four-year survey of tropical fungi in the Caribbean and Central America. So far they alone have discovered more than 100 new species.

C   And of course the role of fungi in the development of various medicines adds to this. Most famously, the fungus Penicillium was refined into penicillin, the first antibiotic effective against bacterial infection.

D   This means that they are seldom in the spotlight. 'We're always trying to drum up support for mushrooms,' said Dr. Czederpiltz. 'But it's an uphill battle. Cute, pretty or furry things tend to get all the attention.'

E   Whatever the real figure, new species are added almost daily to the list of those that have. Last year, one journal, *Mycotaxon*, published details of 258 new or renamed fungi. From 1980 to 1999, an average of 1,100 new species were found and described every year.

F   Their prey are small, fragile and sometimes hidden, so fungi hunters spend a lot of time on their hands and knees in search of finds like that one. 'The tree guys, they'll get a couple kilometers down the trail,' said Dr. Baroni. 'Some days we won't get out of earshot of camp.'

G   Towering palms and strangler figs, their trunks wrapped in a green shag of ferns and mosses, rise and converge in a leafy canopy that keeps the moist forest floor in perpetual dusk. The place is so remote that the British Army's jungle training unit dropped the expedition members and a reporter in by helicopter.

PART 3

You are going to read a newspaper article about a traffic system. For questions 13–19, choose the answer (A, B, C or D) which you think fits best according to the text.

Mark your answers on the separate answer sheet.

Road with no signs

Drachten, The Netherlands. 'I want to take you on a walk,' said Hans Monderman, abruptly stopping his car and striding hatless into the freezing rain. He led the way to a busy intersection in the centre of town, where several odd things soon became clear. Not only was it virtually naked, stripped of all lights, signs and road markings, but there was no division between road and sidewalk. It was basically a bare brick square. But despite the unusual layout, a steady stream of trucks, cars, buses, motorcycles, bicycles and pedestrians moved fluidly and easily, as if directed by an invisible conductor. When Mr Monderman, a traffic engineer and the intersection's proud designer, deliberately failed to look for oncoming traffic before crossing the street, the drivers slowed for him. No one honked or shouted rude words out of the window. 'Who has the right of way?' he asked rhetorically. 'I don't care. People here have to find their own way, negotiate for themselves, use their own brains.'

Used by some 20,000 drivers a day, the intersection is part of a road-design revolution pioneered by the 59-year-old Mr Monderman. His work in Friesland, the district in Northern Holland that includes Drachten, is increasingly seen as the way of the future in Europe. His philosophy is simple, if counter-intuitive. To make communities safer and more appealing, Mr Monderman argues, you should first remove the traditional paraphernalia of their roads – traffic lights and speed signs, the centre lines separating lanes from one another, even the speed bumps, bicycle lanes and pedestrian crossings. In his view, it is only when the road is made more dangerous, when drivers stop looking at signs and start looking at other people, that driving becomes safer. 'All those signs are saying to cars, "This is your space, and we have organized your behaviour so that as long as you behave this way, nothing can happen to you",' Mr Monderman said. 'That is the wrong story.'

The Drachten intersection is an example of the concept of 'shared space', where cars and pedestrians are equal, and the design tells the driver what to do. In Mr Monderman's view, shared-space designs thrive only in conjunction with well-organized, well-regulated highway systems. Variations on the shared-space theme are being tried in Spain, Denmark, Austria, Sweden and Britain, among other places. The European Union has appointed a committee of experts, including Mr Monderman, for a Europe-wide study.

A few years ago, Mr Monderman, now considered one of the field's great innovators, was virtually unknown outside Holland. He was working as a civil engineer, building highways in the 1970s when the Dutch government, alarmed at a sharp increase in traffic accidents, set up a network of traffic-safety offices. Mr Monderman was appointed Friesland's traffic safety officer. In residential communities, Mr Monderman began narrowing the roads and putting in features like trees and flowers, red-brick paving stones and even fountains to discourage people from speeding, following the principle now known as psychological traffic calming, where behaviour follows design. He created his first shared space in a small village where residents were upset at it being used as a daily thoroughfare for 6,000 speeding cars. When he took away the signs, lights and sidewalks, people drove more carefully. Within two weeks, speeds on the road had dropped by more than half. In fact, he said, there has never been a fatal accident on any of his roads.

Mr Monderman concedes that road design can only do so much. It does not change the behaviour, for instance, of the 15 per cent of drivers who will behave badly no matter what the rules are. Recently a group of well-to-do parents asked him to widen the two-lane road leading to their children's school, saying it was too small to accommodate what he derisively calls 'their huge cars'. He refused, saying the fault was not with the road, but with the cars. 'They can't wait for each other to pass?' he asked. 'I wouldn't interfere with the right of people to buy the car they want but nor should the government have to solve the problems they make with their choices.'

13 When the writer first saw the intersection, one thing that struck her was

   A the attractiveness of a square without lights or signs.
   B the extent to which the layout particularly suited pedestrians.
   C the lack of separation between vehicles and pedestrians.
   D the large number of people and vehicles moving in the same direction.

13

14 When Hans Monderman stepped into the road, the writer

   A was surprised by the reaction of drivers to his behaviour.
   B knew that it would be perfectly safe to follow him.
   C had some doubts about his explanation of his behaviour.
   D wondered whether what she witnessed was typical or not.

14

15 Hans Monderman's philosophy is described in the second paragraph as 'counter-intuitive' because

   A it contradicts a lot of evidence about road safety.
   B it appears to involve the possibility of more accidents.
   C it forces drivers to do something they do not wish to do.
   D it might seem to favour the least careful drivers.

15

16 In the third paragraph, the writer says that 'shared space' intersections

   A are not likely to catch on in some countries as much as in others.
   B may be appealing in theory but may have serious drawbacks in practice.
   C can compensate for failings in other aspects of road design.
   D are not claimed to be a solution to road safety issues on their own.

16

17 We are told that when Hans Monderman became a traffic safety officer,

   A his introduction of a shared space had a rapid effect.
   B he made more innovations than the government had envisaged.
   C his initial innovations were not as effective as he had hoped.
   D he had been waiting for the opportunity to introduce shared space design.

17

18 We are told that the request from a particular group of parents to Mr Monderman

   A is typical of the kind of issue that he has to deal with.
   B was something for which he had no sympathy at all.
   C raises a new issue that requires careful consideration.
   D resulted in him making an exception to one of his rules.

18

19 Which of the following best sums up Hans Monderman's view?

   A Telling drivers what to do causes roads to become more dangerous.
   B Roads are safer if drivers are forced to make decisions for themselves.
   C Drivers know more about road safety than most people designing road systems.
   D Drivers welcome any innovations that genuinely contribute to improved road safety.

19

PART 4

You are going to read an article about some children. For questions 20–34, choose from the sections of the article (A–E). The sections may be chosen more than once. When more than one answer is required, these may be given in any order.

Mark your answers on the separate answer sheet.

In which section of the article are the following mentioned?

an example of a sign that has become simpler — 20

the difference between how the deaf children communicate an image and how other people communicate the same image — 21

the fact that the same signs can be used in the communication of a number of ideas — 22

the children's sign language becoming increasingly complex — 23   24

the characteristics of languages in general at different stages of their development — 25

a belief that language is learnt by means of a specific part of the mind — 26   27

an aspect of language learning that children are particularly good at — 28

how regularly the children have been monitored — 29

older children passing their sign language on to younger children — 30

a reason why the children are regarded as being different from any other group of people — 31   32

the reason why the children created a particular sign — 33

opposing views on how people acquire language — 34

DEAF CHILDREN'S LANGUAGE HINTS AT HOW BRAIN WORKS

A A deep insight into the way the brain learns language has emerged from the study of Nicaraguan sign language, invented by deaf children in a Nicaraguan school as a means of communicating among themselves. The finding suggests that the brain naturally breaks complex concepts into smaller components, indicating a dedicated neural machinery for language. The Nicaraguan children are well-known to linguists because they provide an apparently unique example of people inventing a language from scratch. The phenomenon started at a school for special education founded in 1977. Instructors noticed that the deaf children, while absorbing little from their Spanish lessons, had developed a system of signs for talking to one another. As one generation of children taught the system to the next, it evolved from a set of gestures into a far more sophisticated form of communication, and today's 800 users of the language provide a living history of the stages of formation.

B The children have been studied principally by Dr. Judy Kegi, a linguist at the University of Southern Maine, and Dr. Ann Senghas, a cognitive scientist at Columbia University in New York City. In the latest study, published in *Science* magazine, Dr. Senghas shows that the younger children have now decomposed certain gestures into smaller component signs. A hearing person asked to mime a standard story about a cat waddling down a

street will make a single gesture, a downward spiral motion of the hand. But the deaf children have developed two different signs to use in its place. They sign a circle for the rolling motion and then a straight line for the direction of movement. This requires more signing, but the two signs can be used in combination with others to express different concepts. The development is of interest to linguists because it captures a principal quality of human language – discrete elements usable in different combinations – in contrast to the one sound, one meaning of animal communication. 'The regularity she documents here – mapping discrete aspects of the world onto discrete word choices – is one of the most distinctive properties of human language,' said Dr. Steven Pinker, a cognitive scientist at Harvard University.

C When people with no common language are thrown into contact, they often develop an ad hoc language known to linguists as a pidgin language, usually derived from one of the parent languages. Pidgins are rudimentary systems with minimal grammar and utterances. But in a generation or two, the pidgins acquire grammar and become upgraded to what linguists call creoles. Though many new languages have been created by the pidgin-creole route, the

Nicaraguan situation is unique, Dr. Senghas said, because its starting point was not a complex language but ordinary gestures. From this raw material, the deaf children appear to be spontaneously fabricating the elements of language.

D Linguists have been engaged in a longstanding argument as to whether there is an innate, specialized neural machinery for learning language, as proposed by Noam Chomsky of the Massachusetts Institute of Technology, or whether everything is learned from scratch. Dr. Senghas says her finding supports the view that language learning is innate, not purely cultural, since the Nicaraguan children's disaggregation of gestures appears to be spontaneous. Her result also upholds the idea that children play an important part in converting a pidgin into a creole. Because children's minds are primed to learn the rules of grammar, it is thought, they spontaneously impose grammatical structure on a pidgin that doesn't have one.

E The Nicaraguan children are a living laboratory of language generation. Dr. Senghas, who has been visiting their school every year since 1990, said she had noticed how the signs for numbers have developed. Originally the children represented '20' by flicking the fingers of both hands in the air twice. But this cumbersome sign has been replaced with a form that can now be signed with one hand. The children don't care that the new sign doesn't look like a 20, Dr. Senghas said; they just want a symbol that can be signed fast.

Paper 2: Writing (1 hour 30 minutes)

PART 1

You must *answer this question. Write your answer in* 180–220 *words in an appropriate style.*

1   You have seen a request in an English-language magazine for readers to send in articles about the national newspapers in their country and you have decided to write an article for the magazine.
Read the extract from the magazine and the notes you have made for the article. Then, using the information appropriately, write your article for the magazine.

> We're planning to do a series on the media in different countries and for the first part of the series we're going to focus on national newspapers. We'd like you to send us short articles about the national newspapers in your countries. Tell us what kinds of newspaper there are and give us some information about them. And give us your opinions on them too. We'll print a whole section of your articles so that readers can compare the papers in different countries.

NOTES

Possible areas to discuss:

- how many there are (and names)
- which are most popular
- what they contain (serious news, gossip, sport, politics, etc.)
- who reads them (type of person, age, etc.)
- which I read
- what I think of them (interesting, dull, etc.)

Write your article. You should use your own words as far as possible.

PART 2

Write an answer to one of the questions 2–5 in this part. Write your answer in 220–260 words in an appropriate style.

2 You see the following announcement in an international magazine.

PRODUCT REVIEWS WANTED

Have you bought a new product recently, or had one bought for you? Maybe you've just got a new gadget or piece of technology or equipment. It could be something for work or leisure. We'd like to hear what you think of it for our Readers' Reviews Page. Describe the product for readers and give your opinions on it. Do you recommend it? If so, why? If not, why not? Send your review to the address below.

Write your review

3 You see the following notice in the place where you work or study.

ANNIVERSARY EVENT PROPOSALS

As you may know, next year we will have been in existence for 20 years, and at a recent meeting it was decided that we should hold a special event to celebrate this achievement. We're now looking for proposals as to what kind of event to hold. Have you got a good idea for a special event to celebrate our 20th anniversary? Put together a proposal, giving details of your idea and how the event could be organized. We'll consider all the proposals at a meeting next month.

Write your proposal.

4 Your teacher has asked you to write an essay on the following topic.

It is essential that both education and work should be fun. Otherwise, people cannot be expected to learn or work effectively.

Write your essay.

5 Answer one of the following two questions based on your reading of one of the set books.

Either

5(a) Write an essay describing characters in the book who contrast with each other. Describe each one and say how they differ from each other.

Or

5(b) Write an article describing your experience of reading the book. How quickly or slowly did you read it? Did you find it easy or difficult to understand or follow? Did you feel the same about it all the way through or did your feelings about it change as you went through it?

Paper 3: Use of English (1 hour)

PART 1

For questions 1–12, read the text below and decide which answer (A, B, C or D) best fits each gap. There is an example at the beginning (0).

Mark your answers on the separate answer sheet.

Example:

0 **A** notice   **B** regard   **C** look at   **D** stare at

0	A	B	C	D

Disappearing Alaskan seals

On a winter afternoon, a dozen male Northern fur seals are on an island off south-western Alaska. To **0**_____ them, fighting for territory on the rocks, it's hard to imagine that they are at the **1**_____ of a baffling scientific mystery: why is this species beginning to disappear?

These seals – which can weigh up to 270 kilograms – have an important and symbolic **2**_____ in Alaska's history. Their soft and luxurious fur, the coveted prize during the huge commercial sea harvests that were legal here in the Bering Sea through the early 20th century, was once so valuable it **3**_____ Alaska's economy. Starting in the 1950s, for reasons that are **4**_____ because the harvests by then tended to be fairly small, the seal population began a slow decline. But lately it has been falling drastically, declining at an alarming **5**_____ of 6 per cent a year since 1998. From a **6**_____ of more than 2 million in Alaska in 1948, their numbers have fallen to about 1.1 million.

So **7**_____ no one has been able to establish a precise cause for this, although theories **8**_____. The seals' food supply may be **9**_____, or another species may be **10**_____ on the seals – perhaps killer whales, which no longer have as many great whales to eat because of harvesting of those mammals. Some people have suggested that the decline can be **11**_____ to entanglement in fishing nets, but scientists say they doubt that this alone could **12**_____ the recent population decline.

1	**A** middle	**B** centre	**C** inside	**D** focus
2	**A** location	**B** situation	**C** place	**D** spot
3	**A** drove	**B** inspired	**C** motivated	**D** set
4	**A** unclear	**B** unsure	**C** unsettled	**D** undecided
5	**A** speed	**B** pace	**C** scale	**D** rate
6	**A** top	**B** summit	**C** crest	**D** high
7	**A** long	**B** far	**C** on	**D** forth
8	**A** flourish	**B** mushroom	**C** abound	**D** escalate
9	**A** thinner	**B** tighter	**C** slimmer	**D** scarcer
10	**A** preying	**B** devouring	**C** hounding	**D** ravaging
11	**A** designated	**B** attributed	**C** stipulated	**D** consigned
12	**A** reason with	**B** answer to	**C** account for	**D** match up

PART 2

For questions 13–27, read the text below and think of the word which best fits each gap. Use only one word in each gap. There is an example at the beginning (0).

Write your answers IN CAPITAL LETTERS on the separate answer sheet.

Example:

0	L	I	K	E														

In rock'n'roll, older means richer

The universal fantasy about being a rock star, at least the tame part, goes something 0 _____ this: you make wildly popular new music, see 13 _____ likeness splashed across magazine covers, and worry occasionally 14 _____ becoming old. But according to a new list of the fifty top-earning pop stars, old rock stars are enjoying the 15 _____ success. Half the top ten earners are older than fifty, and two are 16 _____ sixty. Only one act has members under thirty.

The annual list reverses the common perception 17 _____ pop music. Not only is it not the province of youth, it's also 18 _____ the province of CD sales, hit songs and music videos. While young stars 19 _____ their turn on the charts, which rank popular artists, songs and albums, the real pop pantheon, 20 _____ seems, is an older group, no 21 _____ producing new hits, but re-enacting songs that are older than many of today's pop idols.

'This always 22 _____ as a shock to fans,' said Joe Levy of *Rolling Stone* magazine. 'The biggest-selling artists aren't the ones who make the most money. The artists learn the hard 23 _____ that money comes from concert tickets and T-shirts, not selling records. That's the lesson – you build a brand over time, and you can sell the brand 24 _____ if you can't sell the albums.' This means that, while it's good to be in demand, it is 25 _____ to be yesterday's in-demand performer. 26 _____ pop music glorifies the young and the new, it actually sells these qualities 27 _____ a discount.

For questions 28–37, read the text below. Use the word given in capitals at the end of some of the lines to form a word that fits in the gap in the same line. There is an example at the beginning (0).

Write your answers IN CAPITAL LETTERS on the separate answer sheet.

Example:

0	R	E	S	I	G	N	A	T	I	O	N							

EXIT INTERVIEWS

If you are thinking of leaving your job, you may think that handing in your letter of 0 _____ is the end of the matter. But an increasing number of companies now conduct 'exit interviews' with staff in an attempt to improve staff retention and communication.   RESIGN

For the employee, an exit interview may feel like an ideal opportunity to rant and rave about every little 28 _____ that has troubled them   ANNOY
since they got the job. But, 29 _____ in mind that you will probably   BEAR
still need a 30 _____ from these people, it is best to avoid getting   REFER
angry or 31 _____ , and just answer the questions as calmly and   EMOTION
with as much 32 _____ as possible.   HONEST

For employers, the exit interview is a rare opportunity to gather some valuable information about the way staff perceive the internal 33 _____   WORK
of the company. 34 _____ employees may not wish to cause   EXIST
35 _____ to the boss or damage their chances of promotion, so are   OFFEND
unlikely to 36 _____ their real feelings about the company. However,   CLOSE
someone who has already resigned is more likely to be 37 _____ when   TRUE
giving their opinions.

PART 4

For questions 38–42, think of one *word only which can be used appropriately in all three sentences. Here is an example (0).*

Example:

0 If you're _____ next weekend, perhaps we could get together then.

This seat is _____ if you want to sit on it.

Feel _____ to stay with us any time you need a place to stay.

Example:

0	F	R	E	E												

Write only the missing word IN CAPITAL LETTERS *on the separate answer sheet.*

---

38 I think she's got a very good _____ of succeeding as a musician because she's very talented.

He took the job because it was his only _____ of earning a living.

By _____ , the two of us happened to be at the airport at exactly the same time.

39 Please _____ the terrible state of this room, I haven't had time to tidy it up.

I know that she's under a lot of pressure, but nothing can _____ her terrible behaviour.

Would you _____ me for a moment – I need to leave the room and make a phone call.

40 Vanessa is tired because she's had a lot of _____ nights recently.

There were lots of _____ arrivals at the party because of traffic problems.

Mike was in his _____ thirties when he finally found a career that he liked.

41 I'm having a party at my _____ next weekend, would you like to come?

If he keeps playing so badly, he will lose his _____ in the team.

This café is a very good _____ for meeting people.

42 I expect we'll _____ again one day, but bye for now.

The company's service didn't _____ my requirements.

You're going to _____ a lot of problems as you go through life.

PART 5

For questions 43–50, complete the second sentence so that it has a similar meaning to the first sentence, using the word given. Do not change the word given. You must use between three and six words, including the word given. Here is an example (0).

Example:

0 I didn't know the way there, so I got lost.

GET

Not _____ there, I got lost.

| 0 | K | N | O | W | I | N | G | | H | O | W | | T | O | | G | E | T |

Write the missing words IN CAPITAL LETTERS on the separate answer sheet.

43 I've just noticed that the car has almost run out of petrol.

HARDLY

I've just noticed that _____ left in the car.

44 I didn't know that cars were so expensive in this country.

IDEA

I _____ so much in this country.

45 Don't get depressed because of such a small problem.

LET

It's such a small problem that you shouldn't _____ down.

46 It is reported that he is now recovering in hospital.

RECOVERY

He is reported _____ in hospital now.

47 Laura's teacher says that she doesn't have a serious enough attitude to her work.

SERIOUSLY

Laura doesn't _____ to her teacher.

48 He lost his job because he couldn't do what was required.

INABILITY

He lost his job because _____ what was required.

49 I haven't got the energy to argue with you.

BOTHERED

I _____ an argument with you.

50 What's confusing you so much?

LOT

What is it that's _____ confusion?

Paper 4: Listening (40 minutes)

PART 1

You will hear three different extracts. For questions 1–6, choose the answer (A, B or C) which fits best according to what you hear. There are two questions for each extract.

Extract One

You hear two people talking about public speaking.

1   Both speakers refer to a feeling of

   A over-confidence.
   B embarrassment.
   C achievement.

        1

2   The two speakers agree that a big problem with speaking in public is

   A losing the audience's attention during a speech.
   B choosing the wrong content for a speech.
   C feeling nervous at the thought of giving a speech.

        2

Extract Two

You hear part of a radio programme about the London Underground.

3   The poster campaign came at a time when

   A various aspects of life in London were changing.
   B many people were reluctant to travel on the Underground.
   C the use of posters for advertising was increasing.

        3

4   What does Zoe say about the content of the posters?

   A It only appealed to a certain type of person.
   B It contrasted with real life for many people.
   C It influenced the lifestyles of some people.

        4

Extract Three

You hear two people discussing the news media.

5   What opinion does the man express about the news media?

   A It doesn't deserve its reputation.
   B It has become more influential.
   C Its standards have risen.

        5

6   The woman mentions medical stories

   A to explain her attitude to the news media.
   B to illustrate the importance of the news media.
   C to describe why people dislike the news media.

        6

You will hear part of a talk about the invention of the microwave oven.
For questions 7–14, complete the sentences.

THE INVENTION OF THE MICROWAVE OVEN

The invention of the microwave oven began when a chocolate peanut bar

[_____ 7] in Percy Spencer's pocket.

Spencer had previously invented a method for [_____ 8] the tubes
used in radar equipment.

Spencer's first experiment involved putting [_____ 9] near to some
radar equipment.

In his next experiment, an egg was put into a kettle and it [_____ 10].

The first microwave oven was set up in [_____ 11] in Boston in 1946.

The first microwave oven got its name as a result of [_____ 12] at
the company.

One problem with the first microwave oven was that [_____ 13] did
not change colour in it.

When a microwave oven that could be placed on top of a [_____ 14]
was produced, sales began to rise.

You will hear a radio interview with someone who has been having ballet lessons. For questions 15–20, choose the answer (A, B, C or D) which fits best according to what you hear.

15 What does Rupert say about the fact that he is doing ballet classes?
    A Other people have ridiculed him for it.
    B He expects to be mocked for it.
    C It is not as unusual as people might think.
    D People may think it isn't really true.

    `15`

16 Rupert says that before he started doing ballet lessons
    A he had been doing routine physical fitness training.
    B his knowledge of ballet had been growing.
    C ballet had taken over from football as his greatest interest.
    D he had been considering doing ballroom dancing again.

    `16`

17 Rupert say that when the idea of ballet lessons was suggested to him,
    A he thought it was a joke.
    B he was unsure exactly what would be involved.
    C he began to have unrealistic expectations of what he could achieve.
    D he initially lacked the confidence to do it.

    `17`

18 One of the advantages of ballet that Rupert mentions is that
    A it leads to fewer injuries than other physical activities.
    B it has both physical and mental effects.
    C it is particularly good for certain parts of the body.
    D it is more interesting than other forms of exercise.

    `18`

19 What does Rupert say about the sessions?
    A The content of them is varied.
    B Some of the movements in them are harder than others for him.
    C All of the movements in them have to be done accurately.
    D They don't all involve basic movements.

    `19`

20 What does Rupert say about his progress at ballet?
    A It has been much more rapid than he had expected.
    B It has made him consider giving up his other training.
    C It has given him greater appreciation of the skills of professionals.
    D It has led him to enrol for certain exams.

    `20`

PART 4

You will hear five short extracts in which people are talking about people they know.

Task one

For questions 21–25, choose from the list A–H the description each speaker gives of the person.

While you listen you must complete both tasks.

A	critical
B	easily influenced
C	tough
D	careless
E	moody
F	cruel
G	arrogant
H	deceitful

Speaker 1   21

Speaker 2   22

Speaker 3   23

Speaker 4   24

Speaker 5   25

Task two

For questions 26–30, choose from the list A–H the feeling each speaker expresses about the person.

A	sympathy
B	confusion
C	loyalty
D	amusement
E	guilt
F	envy
G	fear
H	annoyance

Speaker 1   26

Speaker 2   27

Speaker 3   28

Speaker 4   29

Speaker 5   30

Paper 5: Speaking (15 minutes)

<u>PART 1</u> (3 minutes)

Work / Study

- What's your job / What are you studying?
- Where do you work / study?
- What do you like most and least about your job / course? ..... (Why?)
- Describe the people that you work / study with.
- Would you like to do a different job / study something else? ..... (Why? / Why not?)

Hobbies

- What hobby / hobbies do you have?
- What do you like about your hobby / hobbies?
- What kind of hobbies do your friends and family have?
- Do you think it's important to have a hobby? ..... (Why? / Why not?)
- Which hobbies that people have to do you consider stupid? ..... (Why?)

<u>PART 2</u> (4 minutes)

1 Characters on TV
2 Things that annoy people

Candidate A	Look at the three photographs 1A, 1B and 1C on page 130. They show **scenes from different TV series.**
	Compare two of the photographs and say **what each series might be about, and what the characters might be like.**
	Candidate A talks on his/her own for about 1 minute.
Candidate B	**Which of the series would you prefer to watch, and why?**
	Candidate B talks on his/her own for about 20 seconds.
Candidate B	Look at the three photographs 2A, 2B and 2C on page 130. They show **things that often annoy people.**
	Compare two of the photographs and say **why people find these things annoying, and what can be done about them.**
	Candidate B talks on his/her own for about 1 minute.
Candidate A	**Which of these things annoys you the most, and why?**
	Candidate A talks on his/her own for about 20 seconds.

PARTS 3 AND 4 (8 minutes)

Tourism

PART 3

Look at the pictures on page 131 showing different aspects of tourism.

First, talk to each other about which aspects of tourism each picture shows. Then decide which picture presents the most positive image of tourism and which the most negative.

Candidates A and B discuss this together for about 3 minutes.

PART 4

- What changes have taken place in tourism in recent times?
- Some people say that tourism does more harm than good. Do you agree?
- Which people benefit the most and the least from modern tourism?
- Some people say that because of tourism, countries all over the world are becoming more similar to each other? Do you agree? Is this a desirable development?
- What developments do you think there will be in tourism in the future?

Paper 1: Reading (1 hour 15 minutes)

PART 1

You are going to read three extracts which are all concerned in some way with communication. For questions 1–6, choose the answer (A, B, C or D) which you think fits best according to the text.

Mark your answers on the separate answer sheet.

Extract from a novel

Cuyler Goodwill's longest oration took place in the year 1916 aboard a train traveling between Winnipeg, Manitoba and Bloomington, Indiana, a distance of some thirteen hundred miles. His audience consisted of one person only, his young daughter Daisy, who was then a mere eleven years of age. They traveled, by day, in a first-class lounge car, courtesy of the Indiana Limestone Company, Cuyler Goodwill's new employer. The journey lasted three full days and for all that time the father talked and talked and talked.

A switch had been shifted in his brain, activated, perhaps, by sheer nervousness, at least at first. He had not 'traveled' before. The world's landscape, as glimpsed from the train window, was larger than he had imagined and more densely compacted. The sight filled him with alarm, and also with excitement. He was discomfited to see how easily men (and women as well) stepped from the train to the station platform, from platform to train – with ease, with levity, laughing and talking and greeting each other as though oblivious to the abrupt geographical shifts they were making.

The first day was the worst. He talked wildly, knowing that shortly he and his daughter would be called to the dining car for the second sitting, and he deeply feared this new excitement. Soon after that the sun would sink from view, and he would be confronted by the aberration of a Pullman bed, of the need to arrange his body in a curtained cubicle.

It was against all this terror that he talked and talked.

---

1 It is suggested in the text that Cuyler Goodwill talked so much because

   A he had been denied the opportunity previously.
   B he wanted his daughter to think that he was feeling relaxed.
   C he was undergoing an experience unfamiliar to him.
   D there were a lot of things he wanted to tell his daughter.

[1]

2 When Cuyler Goodwill looked out of the train, he was struck by

   A the differences between people in different places.
   B how casual the behaviour of people he saw was.
   C the variety of scenery at different points on the journey.
   D how much his feelings changed as the journey went on.

[2]

Bad Language

Researchers who study the evolution of language and the psychology of swearing say that cursing is a human universal. Every language or dialect ever studied, living or dead, spoken by millions or by a small tribe, turns out to have its share of forbidden speech. Young children will memorize the illicit inventory long before they can grasp its sense and writers have always constructed their art on its spine.

Other investigators have determined that hearing a curse elicits a literal rise out of people. When electrodermal wires are placed on people's arms and fingertips to study their skin conductance patterns, and the subjects then hear a few obscenities spoken clearly and firmly, participants show signs of instant arousal. Their skin conductance patterns spike, the hairs on their arms rise, their pulse quickens, and their breathing becomes shallow.

Interestingly, said Kate Burridge, a professor of linguistics at Monash University in Melbourne, Australia, a similar reaction occurs among university students and others who pride themselves on being educated, when they listen to bad grammar or slang expressions that they regard as irritating or illiterate. 'People can feel very passionate about language,' she said, 'as though it were a cherished artefact that must be protected at all costs against the depravities of barbarians and lexical aliens.'

3   Which two aspects of swearing are the main focus of the first two paragraphs?

   A people learning how to do it and people disapproving of it

   B people being shocked by it and people getting used to it

   C people being caused to do it and people refusing to do it

   D people doing it and people witnessing others doing it

> 3

4   The Australian professor refers to people who

   A are extremely intolerant of the incorrect use of language.

   B regard other kinds of bad language as even worse than swearing.

   C are aware that their attitude to the correct use of language is unrealistic.

   D feel that their view of bad language is shared by the majority.

> 4

Can animals talk?

The idea that animals have all-but-human mental lives and powers of communication has become fashionable. Since the 1970s, as animal behaviorists have trained apes to make requests by using gestures or symbols, and acousticians have detected that whales and elephants make subsonic calls, suspicions have arisen that animals have more to say than humans realized.

However, Dr. Stephen R. Anderson, a Yale professor of linguistics and psychology, warns against considering any of these behaviors 'language'. Animals may learn to memorize symbols or sounds, he says, but this does not match the complexity of spoken or deaf sign language. 'Chimps do, after a lot of training, learn 200 or more signs. But they seem to top out after a few years. Kids' vocabularies just go on expanding.' Children also perceive that sounds can be joined to form words into sentences, he says, whereas it is not clear that animals do.

Dr. Emily Sue Savage-Rumbaugh, who has worked with apes for 25 years, disagrees with Dr. Anderson. Some bonobos she works with, she says, have been talked to by humans since birth. By pointing to the right symbols, Kanzi, the best among the bonobos, can form sentences like 'Sue chase Kanzi' and 'Kanzi chase Sue', or can hear the English words 'Get the tomato that is in the microwave' and fetch the tomato.

Linguists have been accused of moving the standard on their definition of language even higher, so it can never be met. They will always deny that animals can talk, Dr Savage-Rumbaugh argues, 'because it doesn't fit comfortably with their view of the universe.' Dr. Anderson replies that he has 'no desire to deny speech even to the cockroach', but he doesn't think non-humans have the potential.

5   The debate described in the text centres on

   A   how much training animals need to be given in order to acquire language.
   B   whether certain animals can acquire language but others can't.
   C   what can genuinely be considered to be language.
   D   whether evidence of animal use of language is truthful or not.

5

6   Dr Anderson says that his views on the subject

   A   have changed as a result of his work.
   B   are not prejudiced.
   C   are likely to cause controversy.
   D   have relevance to the teaching of language.

6

PART 2

You are going to read a newspaper article about robots. Six paragraphs have been removed from the article. Choose from the paragraphs A–G the one which fits each gap (7–12). There is one extra paragraph which you do not need to use.

Mark your answers on the separate answer sheet.

A MAN WHO KNOWS HOW TO BATTLE ROBOTS

In the 2004 movie *I, Robot*, robots rise up against humanity. In the classic sci-fi thriller *Blade Runner*, a bounty hunter must exterminate intelligent androids that are both deadly and very unhappy with their creators. Even in 1920, when the playwright Karel Capek gave English speakers the Czech word *robota* (labourer) in his play *R.U.R.*, the androids at Rossum's Universal Robots were bent on wiping out the human race. 'If popular culture has taught us anything,' Daniel H. Wilson says, 'it is that some day mankind must face and destroy the growing robot menace.' Luckily, Mr Wilson is just the guy to help us do it. In his new book *How to Survive a Robot Uprising*, Dr Wilson offers detailed – and hilariously serious – advice on the subject.

7

If all this fails, reasoning with a robot may work, Dr Wilson says, but emotional appeals will fall on deaf sensors. Should you prevail, he offers in a grim addendum: 'Have no mercy. Your enemy doesn't.'

8

Unlike Bill Joy, co-founder of Sun Microsystems, who has written about what he perceives as the potential robot menace, Dr Wilson does not view robotics as contributing to what Mr Joy called 'the further perfection of pure evil'.

9

So he decided to examine popular culture – science fiction books and movies, even *R.U.R.* – for scenarios of robot uprisings. Then he talked to researchers around the world about how plausible they might be, and about the state of robot technology generally. He found them 'surprisingly eager to put themselves into these made-up situations'.

10

For example, he recalls, when he asked his adviser at Carnegie Mellon, Chris Atkeson, how large a walking robot could be, the question provoked a lively discussion in the lab, ending with a consensus that they could probably be no taller than a telegraph pole.

11

'But it turned out very nicely,' Dr Atkeson says. People will pick it up because it is funny – 'and then you have an opportunity to educate them. It's a robotics primer.'

12

And in his own life, he says, he does not feel too threatened by robots. 'If you want to worry about something, worry about humans,' says Dr Wilson, who is 27. 'Humans are much more dangerous.'

A   But if the scenarios are outlandish (so far), the information is real. By the time readers have absorbed all the possible technological advances rebellious robots could exploit, they have taken a tour of the world's robotic labs, where, Dr Wilson maintains, all the techniques and tools in the book already exist or are under development.

B   In any event, Dr Wilson is hardly heeding his own warnings. In fact, he is looking for a job in commercial robotics research.

C   In fact, he says, he wrote the book out of annoyance with the way the popular media portrayed robots. 'I was kind of tired of them getting a bad rap,' he says. 'In movies and in television, the robots are always the bad guys.'

D   And that's not all there is to it. Dr Wilson is currently waiting for the movie company Paramount Pictures to decide whether to film a sci-fi comedy out of the book. Certainly, he thinks it has all the right ingredients.

E   This includes evading hostile swarms of robot insects (don't try to fight – 'loss of an individual robot is inconsequential to the swarm'); outsmarting your 'smart' house (be suspicious if the house suggests you test the microwave by putting your head in it); and surviving hand-to-hand combat with a humanoid (smear yourself in mud to disguise your distinctive human thermal signature and go for the 'eyes' – its cameras).

F   When Dr Wilson started writing the book, he was still a graduate student. Some of the people he consulted were nervous about it, in part because they feared other researchers would not respect anyone who took such a comical approach to his work and then presented it to a popular audience. Dr Wilson himself said he feared some readers might not get the joke.

G   But, despite this statement, he is no foe of robots, he says. A native of Tulsa, Oklahoma, he earned his doctorate in robotics at Carnegie Mellon in Pittsburgh, a major centre for research in the field, just as his book was coming out late last year.

You are going to read a newspaper article about management. For questions 13–19, choose the answer (A, B, C or D) which you think fits best according to the text.

Mark your answers on the separate answer sheet.

Simply ticking the boxes isn't enough

I have been asked what I think about the idea of 'Investing in People'. The best answer I can give is that I think that what it tries to achieve – basically making the link between business improvement and focusing on the needs of the people who work for an organization – is great. My problem is with organizations who subscribe to it as a way to help them 'get better', when they don't bother to understand where they went wrong in the first place. They need to ask what explicit and implicit policies and procedures they have in place that prevent their people from being able to do the right thing for the right reasons.

I am sure that there are managers out there who don't know any better, and assume that to manage they simply need to put pressure on their people to perform. But people don't demonstrate high performance because they are told to. They do it because they see the need to do it, and make the choice to do so. They do it because they are connected to the business goals and they see how their contributions can help achieve them. Such managers may tell themselves they can put a 'tick' in the 'we care about people' box. But simply putting ticks in boxes is no good if it doesn't reflect reality.

I know of a company that was so concerned that its people were doing the 'right thing' that it put in place a series of metrics to measure their effectiveness. So far, so good. But one of the objectives – making successful sales calls – manifested itself in the metric 'Number of potential customers seen in one day'. The sales people obviously focused their efforts on going from one customer's office to another, and not on closing deals. Instead of the employees becoming more effective, they focused on getting the boxes ticked. Good intent; poor thinking.

Another company wanted to improve the speed with which it was able to introduce new products. Competition was beating it to the market place, and consequently the company was losing market share. Senior management sent out the message to reduce the time spent in getting products into customers' hands, with the explanation that they couldn't afford delays. This was a relatively easy task, especially since the time spent testing the products was cut in half to accomplish the time reduction. The result was new products were introduced in less time than those of the competition – but soon rejected by customers for poor quality. Good intent; reckless implementation.

A third company I know is trying hard to help employees see that they have some control over their future. The company instituted a programme with a title like 'Creating our own future' or something like that. A good idea; get the people involved in the future of the company. But instead of the employees becoming motivated to contribute, they saw it as a hollow exercise on the part of senior management who, in the past, had paid little attention to anything other than getting the job done so they could report great earnings. Yes, the programme was a big 'tick the box' effort, but that was all it was in the minds of the people that it was designed for.

A final example is of a company that brought in one of these 'Investing in People' programmes to change the way the company was run. Assessors were running around like crazy, helping managers examine how they managed. They told managers how they could manage better. And when the programme was over, the company was able to say they had done it – it had invested in its people and life was now good. But the managers simply went back to business as usual. After all, the assessors were gone, and they had targets to hit.

All these examples are representative of senior management who see the need to improve things in their organization, but don't see how to do it. For a start, a programme targeted at improving things is only as good as management's ability to motivate their people. And when the employees simply see the programme as a box-ticking exercise, then it's hopeless. If a company is going to go through the effort implied in investing in people, it should make it worthwhile. Defaulting on the choice to improve the decision-making process by going through the motions is as lame as senior management saying their people's poor performance is not the senior management's fault.

13 The writer thinks that putting the concept of 'Investing in People' into practice
   A frequently results in confusion among the people it is supposed to help.
   B involves more effort than some organizations are prepared to make.
   C may create problems where previously there had not been any problems.
   D is something that some organizations should not attempt to do.

   13

14 The writer's main point in the second paragraph is that the performance of employees
   A may be very good even if management is poor.
   B cannot be accurately measured by any box-ticking exercise.
   C is related to their knowledge of the organization as a whole.
   D is not as unpredictable as some managers believe it to be.

   14

15 What point does the writer make about the first company he describes?
   A It was not really interested in measuring the effectiveness of employees.
   B The targets that it set for staff were unrealistic.
   C It failed to understand the real needs of its employees.
   D The data that it collected did not measure what it was supposed to measure.

   15

16 What point does the writer make about the second company he describes?
   A It made what should have been an easy task into a complicated one.
   B It failed to foresee the consequences of an instruction.
   C It misunderstood why a new approach was required.
   D It refused to take into account the views of employees.

   16

17 What does the writer say about the programme introduced by the third company he mentions?
   A Employees did not believe that it had been introduced for their benefit.
   B Employees felt that it was in fact a way of making their jobs even harder.
   C The reason given for introducing it was not the real reason why it was introduced.
   D It was an inappropriate kind of programme for this particular organization.

   17

18 The writer says that the programme in his final example
   A was too demanding for managers to maintain long-term.
   B was treated as a self-contained exercise by managers.
   C involved some strange ideas on how managers could improve.
   D caused managers to believe that their previous methods had been better.

   18

19 The writer's main criticism of senior management in the final paragraph is that they
   A do not involve employees enough in how their organizations are run.
   B blame employees when programmes for improving their organizations
       prove unsuccessful.
   C are not genuinely committed to the idea of improving their organizations.
   D keep changing their minds about how best to improve their organizations.

   19

PART 4

You are going to read an article about various birds in Britain. For questions 20–34, choose from the birds (A–D). The birds may be chosen more than once.

Mark your answers on the separate answer sheet.

Of which bird are the following stated?

On a number of occasions, fears concerning it have been expressed.		20
Some birds that were introduced did not survive.		21
Further attempts to increase its numbers were made once initial attempts had proved successful.		22
Its population growth is a reflection of how tough it is.		23
It is known for following a routine.		24
Its situation was improved by an initiative that has been referred to as unique.		25
There is statistical evidence to support the view that it is a very popular bird.		26
There was a particular period when its population plummeted.		27
A criticism could be made of its physical appearance.		28
It can easily be identified by its outline.		29
A common perception of it has proved inaccurate.		30
Growth in its numbers has been much more gradual than desired.		31
There is reason to believe that its progress in a particular region will be maintained.		32
Measures taken in the running of a certain type of countryside have assisted in the growth of its population.		33
Even though its population has fallen, it can frequently be seen in various particular locations.		34

Winged winners and losers

Birds in Britain come under scrutiny in a massive new study, *Birds Britannica*. A record of the avian community in the 21st century, it reveals a continually evolving pattern. Mark Cocker, the principal author of the tome, selects some cases

A Red Kite

The red kite's recent rise from a mere handful to several thousands is among the great stories of modern conservation. Testimony to its flagship status is a recent Royal Society for the Protection of Birds poll which ranked it with the golden eagle and song thrush in the nation's list of favourite birds.

The dramatic spread has hinged on a reintroduction scheme at six sites in England and Scotland using kites originally taken from Spain and Sweden. The English releases began in the Chilterns in 1989 and when these had achieved a healthy population, subsequent introductions were made in Northamptonshire and Yorkshire using mainly English birds. The Scottish releases in the 1980s and 1990s have resulted in populations totalling more than 50 pairs. Altogether there are now about 3,000 kites in Britain.

The formation of a 'Kite committee' by members of the British Ornithologists Club in 1903 was central to the bird's recovery. It endured for 90 years and has been described as being 'without parallel in the annals of bird protection anywhere in the world'.

B Dartford Warbler

This highly-attractive bird is confined to just five Western European countries as well as the north African littoral, and has the smallest world range of any of our breeding birds. It is also a highly-sedentary bird and a major cause of decline is its great susceptibility to the cold. The worst case occurred in the two successive hard winters of 1961 and 1962 when the numbers fell from 450 pairs to just 10.

Memories of this calamitous decrease, coupled with the bird's own tiny size and seeming delicacy, have cemented our sense of an overarching vulnerability. It is one of the best British examples where a species' local rarity has been assumed to equal almost constitutional weakness. Typical of our pessimism was a 1960s prediction that its breeding range would be virtually restricted to the New Forest 'in the foreseeable future'. There was a similar anxiety in the proposal to trap large numbers ahead of severe winter weather so that they could be safely released the following spring.

All the caution is perfectly understandable as an expression of our protective instincts towards a much-loved bird. Yet it sits oddly with the warbler's continuing rise and expansion to a population of 1,925 pairs by the year 2000. It has undoubtedly been helped by mild winters as well as the intensive management and protection of England's lowland heath. Yet the Dartford Warbler's recent history illustrates how easy it is to underestimate the resilience of a small rare bird.

C White-tailed Eagle

It is difficult to judge which is the more exciting conservation achievement – the reintroduction of this magnificent bird or of red kites. By wingspan and weight, this is the largest eagle in Europe and one of the biggest of all birds in Britain. However, if the species itself is on a grand scale, the size of the reintroduced population is tiny and the pace of increase agonizingly slow. Almost 30 years after the species was first released, there are just 23 pairs holding territory, and from 17 occupied eyries in 2001, no more than 11 young fledged.

The project involved a remarkable team effort by various UK environmental groups, as well as the Norwegian conservationists who organized the capture of the donated birds. Between 1975 and 1985, they released 82 eagles (39 males and 43 females) from a special holding area on the Inner Hebridean island of Rhum. Eight were later recovered dead, but in 1983 came the first breeding attempt.

Two years later, a pair of white-tailed eagles produced the first British-born chick in 69 years and every subsequent breeding season has seen a small incremental improvement. There is now an established breeding nucleus spread between the islands of Skye and Mull as well as the adjacent mainland, and their recent history suggests that the white-tailed eagle's increase will continue throughout north-west Scotland.

D Spotted Flycatcher

Even the greatest fans of this lovely bird, with its mouse-grey upper parts and whitish breast and belly, would have to admit that it is rather drab. They have no more than a thin, squeaky, small song. However, spotted flys compensate with enormous character.

The birds are instantly recognizable because of their large-headed, top-heavy shape that is distinctive even in silhouette, and by the habit of returning to the same perch after their agile, twisting, aerial sallies for insects.

They are adept at catching large species such as day-flying moths, butterflies, bees and wasps, whose stings they remove by thrashing the victim against the perch. Their specialized diet means that they are among the latest spring migrants to return and are now in serious decline because of half a century of pesticide use. In the past 25 years, their numbers have declined by almost 80 per cent, but they are still sufficiently numerous (155,000 pairs) to be familiar and are often birds of large gardens, churchyards or around farm buildings.

Paper 2: Writing (1 hour 30 minutes)

PART 1

*You **must** answer this question. Write your answer in 180–220 words in an appropriate style.*

1   You recently spent a week at an adventure sports centre. A friend is thinking of going to the same place and has contacted you about it.
Read the extract from your friend's letter to you and the extracts from the diary you kept when you were at the adventure centre. Then, using the information appropriately, write a letter to your friend, giving the advice and information your friend wants.

... So I'm thinking of going to the same place. You haven't told me much about it — what's it like? Would you recommend it for me? I've got the brochure and it sounds really exciting. Of course, I'm not as brave as you, but I'd like to do something challenging and see how I get on. Do you think I'd find some of the activities too scary? I guess it's all safe, isn't it?

Monday   *Assault course — climb up this, crawl through that — exhausting but fun. I'm glad I'm fit enough for all this!*

Tuesday
Rock climbing — great fun! Couldn't do it at first but got the hang of it eventually.

Wednesday
Canoeing — quite scary but felt safe because the teacher was with me all the time.

Thursday
Camp in the woods — lots of laughter as we tried to put up tents.

Friday
In groups, build a raft to get across the river. My group's was the only one that worked OK!

Saturday
Diving — each person with a qualified teacher, but I panicked a bit and gave up.

Sunday
Last day — tired but had great time — and made a few new friends. I've learnt things I couldn't do before — great teachers.

Write your **letter**. You do not need to include postal addresses. You should use your own words as far as possible.

Write an answer to one of the questions 2–5 in this part. Write your answer in 220–260 words in an appropriate style.

2   You have been asked to write a contribution for an English-language guidebook for your city or region. You have been asked to write a piece for a section of the book about notable buildings in your city or region. You have been told that your piece should include a description of one building, details about visiting it and opinions on it.

Write your guidebook contribution.

3   You see the following announcement about a competition in an international magazine.

> ## THE THREE POSSESSIONS THAT MATTER MOST TO YOU
>
> Win a holiday for two in this month's writing competition. We want you to tell us which three of your possessions are most precious to you. What are the three things you simply couldn't be without? Give details of what they are and when or how you got them. And tell us why they matter so much to you.

Write your competition entry.

4   As part of an exchange programme, you recently spent a week staying in another country with someone who had previously stayed with you as part of the same exchange programme. You have been asked to write a report on your experience. Your report should include where you went and who you stayed with, and what you did during your visit. It should also include a comparison between your visit and the person's previous stay with you, as well as any points you wish to make about the exchange programme in general.

Write your report.

5   Answer one of the following two questions based on your reading of one of the set books.

Either

5(a) Write a letter to a magazine suggesting that they should choose the book as one of their Books Of The Month. Explain why you are recommending it and who it would appeal to.

Or

5(b) Write an essay about how realistic you feel that the characters and events in the book are. Explain why you think they are realistic and compare them with real people and events.

Paper 3: Use of English (1 hour)

PART 1

For questions 1–12, read the text below and decide which answer (A, B, C or D) best fits each gap. There is an example at the beginning (0).

Mark your answers on the separate answer sheet.

Example:

0 **A** declared   **B** identified   **C** defined   **D** announced

0	**A**	**B**	**C**	**D**

An artist whose ego obscured his talent

Having 0_____ himself a genius while in his twenties, Salvador Dalí 1_____ to promote this notion with such relentless conviction that the egotist eventually overshadowed the artist. By the time he died in 1989, leaving hundreds of signed sheets of paper to give 2_____ to a fake Dalí industry, many in the art world had 3_____ against him.

Yet Dalí never came to 4_____ his popular appeal. Although he was 5_____ from the Surrealist Movement in 1939, he remained the best-known Surrealist. And even after Abstract Expressionism and Pop Art had taken the 6_____ of Surrealism, a major Dalí exhibition in Paris in 1979 still 7_____ 800,000 visitors. Today, among 20th-century artists, his renown could be said to be 8_____ only by Picasso's.

Dalí emerged as a 9_____ figure in Surrealism in the late 1920s. In the mid-1930s, he took Surrealism to the United States and he became so well known there that he was on the cover of *Time* magazine in 1936. He was the first in the group to 10_____ rich from his paintings. Dalí 11_____ his immense popularity, dabbling in 12_____ business and selling his works and image at great profit.

1 **A** came about   **B** brought off   **C** went on   **D** got ahead

2 **A** rise   **B** lead   **C** effect   **D** source

3 **A** fallen   **B** set   **C** run   **D** turned

4 **A** cease   **B** drop   **C** lose   **D** halt

5 **A** evicted   **B** rid   **C** thrown   **D** expelled

6 **A** place   **B** spot   **C** space   **D** role

7 **A** drew   **B** caught   **C** fetched   **D** grasped

8 **A** overstepped   **B** exceeded   **C** towered   **D** overpowered

9 **A** chief   **B** primary   **C** central   **D** focal

10 **A** grow   **B** make   **C** go   **D** move

11 **A** delighted   **B** rejoiced   **C** thrilled   **D** relished

12 **A** fun   **B** show   **C** play   **D** light

PART 2

For questions 13–27, read the text below and think of the word which best fits each gap. Use only one *word in each gap. There is an example at the beginning (0).*

Write your answers IN CAPITAL LETTERS *on the separate answer sheet.*

Example:

0	A	S											

TRIATHLETES

Stuart Hayes had launched himself on a promising career **0**_____ a swimmer when something odd happened **13**_____ him at the local pool. Flogging up and down for the umpteenth time, he suddenly realized **14**_____ bored he had become with the monotony. Wasn't there a more interesting way of **15**_____ sporty, for heaven's sake? There was **16**_____ there is: the colour, sweat and sheer emotion of triathlons. On August 5 and 6, Stuart, 27, will join almost 10,000 athletes in the London Triathlon, the biggest event of **17**_____ kind in the world.

Triathlons are **18**_____ but boring. Combining swimming, cycling and running in one physical onslaught, they offer huge variety within a single racing framework. The classic Olympic distances are a 1,500 m swim, followed by a 40 km bike ride and a 10 km run. Hayes, a world-class triathlete, won last year's London Triathlon in **19**_____ impressive 1 hour 47 minutes. 'The worst part is the last 5 km of the run – you're starting to get really fatigued by **20**_____,' he says. So why does he **21**_____ it? He shrugs. 'It's interesting.'

In Britain, the sport is growing **22**_____ 10 per cent a year. 'People are moving away **23**_____ just running, and are looking for new challenges,' says Nick Rusling, event director for the London Triathlon. 'Triathlons are a **24**_____ deal more interesting to train for and you can vary training to fit busy lifestyles, swimming in your lunch break and **25**_____ on. On top of **26**_____, people are much more aware of their bodies. They know running is potentially bad **27**_____ the joints. A triathlon is actually very easy and very smooth, particularly the cycle and swim.'

For questions 28–37, read the text below. Use the word given in capitals at the end of some of the lines to form a word that fits in the gap in the same line. There is an example at the beginning (0).

Write your answers IN CAPITAL LETTERS on the separate answer sheet.

Example:

0	W	I	N	N	E	R							

RESTAURANT OF THE YEAR

One more chance! That's all we're giving you to tell us about your

favourite restaurant and boost its chances of becoming the **0** _____   WIN

of our Restaurant of the Year competition. This is the last time the

official **28** _____ form will appear in the paper and next Thursday   NOMINATE

is the final date for **29** _____ of completed forms.   RECEIVE

　　Over the past few weeks we have been swamped by a paper mountain

as **30** _____ across the city jot down the compelling reasons why   DINE

they believe their **31** _____ restaurant should definitely win our   CHOOSE

hotly **32** _____ competition.   CONTEST

　　So far we have received more than 400 **33** _____ forms with more   ENTER

than 30 restaurants nominated. These votes have been **34** _____   EVEN

spread, which makes the last week even more crucial than usual, as we

aim to find the top three to go forward to our grand final.

　　Once the **35** _____ has passed, our judges will sit down and count   DEAD

all the forms. The three restaurants which receive the most votes will

then be visited by the judges. These visits will of course be

36 _____ , so the restaurants themselves will not know that the   ANNOUNCE

judges are there. After their visits, the judges will make their final

decision over who wins the **37** _____ title Restaurant of the Year.   PRESTIGE

For questions 38–42, think of one word only which can be used appropriately in all three sentences. Here is an example (0).

Example:

0   If you're _____ next weekend, perhaps we could get together then.

   This seat is _____ if you want to sit on it.

   Feel _____ to stay with us any time you need a place to stay.

Example:

| 0 | F | R | E | E | | | | | | | | | |

Write only the missing word IN CAPITAL LETTERS on the separate answer sheet.

---

38 I might be _____ about this, but I think you're making a terrible mistake.

   This is the _____ time to discuss such an important matter – I'm much too busy.

   Do you agree that it's morally _____ to cheat other people?

39 If you go to the top of that hill, you get an incredible _____ of the whole city.

   In my _____, this problem is not as serious as you say it is.

   In _____ of the cost involved, we decided not to go ahead with the plan.

40 I'm going to _____ her to a special meal in an expensive restaurant for her birthday.

   Paul is an unpopular boss because he tends to _____ his employees very badly.

   The doctors are not quite sure of the best way to _____ her illness.

41 Is that story _____ or did you make it up?

   He's a _____ friend and I trust him completely.

   What you've said is _____ but it doesn't change my opinion at all.

42 The latest _____ of the magazine includes interviews with all sorts of celebrities.

   This is a very important _____ and we should discuss it seriously.

   When she decided to leave the job, money wasn't the _____ – she left because of the hours.

For questions 43–50, complete the second sentence so that it has a similar meaning to the first sentence, using the word given. Do not change the word given. You must use between three and six words, including the word given. Here is an example (0).

Example:

0   I didn't know the way there, so I got lost.

   GET

   Not _____ there, I got lost.

0	K	N	O	W	I	N	G		H	O	W		T	O		G	E	T

Write the missing words IN CAPITAL LETTERS on the separate answer sheet.

43   It took me some time to understand fully what happened.

   WHILE

   It was _____ understood what had happened.

44   There's no point arguing about this small detail, in my opinion.

   WORTH

   This small detail _____, in my opinion.

45   If your order is delayed, we will contact you.

   DELAY

   Should _____ to your order, we will contact you.

46   He didn't try to help me at all.

   EFFORT

   He _____ any help at all.

47   The two situations are completely different.

   COMMON

   The two situations don't _____ each other.

48   Can I speak to you privately for a few minutes?

   WORD

   Can I _____ you for a few minutes?

49   I was amazed because there were no problems throughout the holiday.

   WENT

   To _____ wrong throughout the holiday.

50   I have no intention of doing another kind of job.

   DREAM

   I _____ other kind of job.

Paper 4: Listening (40 minutes)

PART 1

You will hear three different extracts. For questions 1–6, choose the answer (A, B or C) which fits best according to what you hear. There are two questions for each extract.

Extract One

You hear part of a radio programme about a famous London hotel.

1 The presenter's aim in her introduction is to
   A correct misunderstandings about the Grand.
   B provide factual information about the Grand.
   C encourage listeners to go to the Grand.

[1]

2 What is the manager's attitude towards the customers?
   A He wishes that more of them were not rich people.
   B He treats them all in the same way, regardless of who they are.
   C He always knows instantly what category they belong to.

[2]

Extract Two

You hear two presenters talking on a science programme.

3 The male presenter says that the research produced data on
   A the period of time that some teaspoons were missing.
   B how quickly a certain number of teaspoons disappeared.
   C where disappearing teaspoons had gone.

[3]

4 The female presenter says that disappearing teaspoons is a topic which
   A has produced some interesting theories.
   B concerns a growing phenomenon.
   C has no great significance.

[4]

Extract Three

You hear two people talking about popular music.

5 The woman's main point is that
   A it is no longer possible to create genuinely original popular music.
   B all modern popular music is a poor imitation of older music.
   C popular music has always been an overrated form of music.

[5]

6 What does the woman say about modern performers?
   A They are not interested in the views of older people.
   B They are taking advantage of their audience.
   C They are influenced without realizing it.

[6]

You will hear part of a talk about a common psychological phenomenon.
For questions 7–14, complete the sentences.

DÉJÀ VU

Facts about déjà vu

An example of something that can cause a feeling of déjà vu is the sound made by a
[7   ] .

Surveys show that déjà vu has been experienced by approximately
[8   ] of adults.

Surveys show that people who frequently [9   ] experience
déjà vu more often than others.

Surveys show that déjà vu is most frequently experienced during the period of
[10   ] .

Experiments on déjà vu

In the experiments, students were asked to find a small [11   ] of
one colour or another in various photographs.

Some of the photographs showed [12   ] at the two universities.

Two weeks later, the students were shown the same photographs, but the
[13   ] had been changed.

Some students said that they had been to a [14   ] at a university
that they had in fact never visited.

You will hear a radio discussion about writing a novel. For questions 15–20, choose the answer (A, B, C or D) which fits best according to what you hear.

15 What does Louise say about Ernest Hemingway's advice to writers?
 A It is useful to a certain extent.
 B It applies only to inexperienced novelists.
 C It wasn't intended to be taken seriously.
 D It might confuse some inexperienced novelists.

15 ☐

16 Louise says that you need to get feedback when you
 A have not been able to write anything for some time.
 B are having difficulty organizing your ideas.
 C are having contrasting feelings about what you have written.
 D have finished the book but not shown it to anyone.

16 ☐

17 Louise says that you should get feedback from another writer because
 A it is easy to ignore criticism from people who are not writers.
 B another writer may be kinder to you than friends and relatives.
 C it is hard to find other people who will make an effort to help you.
 D another writer will understand what your intentions are.

17 ☐

18 What does Louise regard as useful feedback?
 A a combination of general observations and detailed comments
 B both identification of problems and suggested solutions
 C comments focusing more on style than on content
 D as many points about strengths as weaknesses

18 ☐

19 What does Louise say about the people she gets feedback from?
 A Some of them are more successful than her.
 B She doesn't only discuss writing with them.
 C She also gives them feedback on their work.
 D It isn't always easy for her to get together with them.

19 ☐

20 One reaction to feedback that Louise mentions is that
 A it is justified but would require too much effort to act on.
 B it focuses on unimportant details rather than key issues.
 C it has been influenced by reading other people's novels.
 D it is not suggesting that major changes to the novel are required.

20 ☐

PART 4

You will hear five short extracts in which people are talking about events they attended.

Task one

For questions 21–25, choose from the list A–H the event each speaker is talking about.

Task two

For questions 26–30, choose from the list A–H what happened according to each speaker.

While you listen you must complete both tasks.

A a concert	A It wasn't well-attended.
B a meeting	B I hardly knew anyone.
C a birthday party	C It ended early.
D a school reunion	D I was treated badly.
E a funeral	E There was an argument.
F a leaving party	F I left before the end.
G a wedding	G Everyone enjoyed themselves.
H a demonstration	H I couldn't focus on the event.

Speaker 1		21	Speaker 1	26
Speaker 2		22	Speaker 2	27
Speaker 3		23	Speaker 3	28
Speaker 4		24	Speaker 4	29
Speaker 5		25	Speaker 5	30

Paper 5: Speaking (15 minutes)

> **English language**
>
> - How long have you been learning English, and why have you been learning it?
> - How have you been learning the language?
> - Why is learning English useful or important to you?
> - What aspects of learning English have you found most and least enjoyable? ..... (Why?)
> - What reasons do other people have for learning English?
>
> **Daily life**
>
> - How does a typical day for you start?
> - What do you like most and least about a typical day for you?
> - Which person / people do you usually see every day?
> - Do you keep a diary? If so, what do you write in it? If not, why not?
> - What meals do you have each day, and when?

PART 2 (4 minutes)

1 Glamorous lives
2 Learning a skill

> | Candidate A | Look at the three photographs 1A, 1B and 1C on page 132. They show **people with careers that are considered exciting or glamorous.** |
> | --- | --- |
> | | Compare two of the photographs and say **what you think each person's life might be like, and what each person's personality might be like.** |
> | | *Candidate A talks on his/her own for about 1 minute.* |
> | Candidate B | **Which of the people would you most or least like to be, and why?** |
> | | *Candidate B talks on his/her own for about 20 seconds.* |
> | Candidate B | Look at the three photographs 2A, 2B and 2C on page 132. They show **people taking classes in order to learn a skill.** |
> | | Compare two of the photographs and say **why the people might be taking the classes, and what might be involved in learning each skill.** |
> | | *Candidate B talks on his/her own for about 1 minute.* |
> | Candidate A | **Which of the skills have you learnt, or would you most like to have, and why?** |
> | | *Candidate A talks on his/her own for about 20 seconds.* |

Young people

PART 3

Look at the pictures on page 133 showing different images of young people.

First, talk to each other about what the young people in each picture are doing. Then decide which picture is most typical of young people today.

Candidates A and B discuss this together for about 3 minutes.

PART 4

- Some people say that life is easier today for young people than it used to be. Do you agree? ..... (Why? / Why not?)
- What things do you think that all young people should be able to have and to do?
- What kind of things are expected of young people today, and why? Are these expectations fair? ..... (Why? / Why not?)
- How much influence do you think young people's families have on them? Do you think that their friends have more influence on them? ..... (Why? / Why not?)
- What kind of problems do young people typically have today? What causes these problems?

Paper 1: Reading (1 hour 15 minutes)

You are going to read three extracts which are all concerned in some way with attitudes. For questions 1–6, choose the answer (A, B, C or D) which you think fits best according to the text.

Mark your answers on the separate answer sheet.

Patience is almost a thing of the past

Young British people have a 'won't wait' mentality which means that almost £400 million in uncashed cheques is sitting in their wallets because they cannot be bothered to pay them in, a survey shows. Those aged between 18 and 29 habitually carry cheques around in their pockets and handbags because they cannot endure queuing at a bank. Their aversion to waiting means that they also avoid visits to the doctor, dentist and even the hairdresser. Two fifths of young adults would forgo a trip to the doctor simply because they could not bear to wait for an appointment and a sixth admitted that they have become ill as a result. Three in ten of the same age said that they did not have time to go to the dentist. More than a third said they would endure long hair or an unflattering style rather than wait for an appointment at a hairdresser's.

This 'won't wait' attitude also affects their social conscience, with one in six freely admitting that they did not give blood because the process took too long. Five per cent said they were too impatient to get married, preferring to stay single because the process was too lengthy. A fifth would abandon a full supermarket trolley at the sight of a lengthy queue at the checkout.

The study found that 29 per cent regarded queuing as an 'absolute waste of time', while one in 20 completely refused to do it. One of the researchers said: 'Being so spoilt for speed, we have lost the trademark British patience. The image of the queuing Englishman has been truly consigned to the past.'

---

1 One thing the study revealed was that young British people

  A realize that their impatience is hard to justify.
  B believe that their impatience is widely shared.
  C are unconcerned about the consequences of their impatience.
  D are embarrassed about the extent of their impatience.

`1`

2 The purpose of the text is to

  A regret a social trend.
  B criticize a social trend.
  C ridicule a social trend.
  D point out a social trend.

`2`

Extract from a novel

In his youth, he had considered himself an intensely political man. He had joined and supported a party, rejoiced in its triumphs, convinced that its accession to power would bring his country closer to social justice. His disillusionment had not been swift, though it had been hastened by the presence of his wife, who had reached a state of political despair and black cynicism well before he allowed himself to follow her lead. He had denied, both in word and in belief, the first accusations of dishonesty and endemic corruption against the men he had been sure would lead the nation to a bright and just future. But then he had looked at the evidence against them, not as a true believer but as a policeman, and his certainty of their guilt had been immediate.

Since then, he had stayed clear of politics entirely, bothering to vote only because to do so set

an example for his children, not because he now believed it could make any difference. In the years during which his cynicism had grown, his former friendships with politicians had languished, and his dealings with them had become formal rather than cordial.

3 **What do we learn about the character's change in attitude towards politicians?**

A It only happened when he took a professional view of their behaviour.
B It resulted from a good deal of persuasion from his wife.
C It began with him doubting that what he was saying about them was true.
D It was something that he wished had happened earlier.

3

4 **What happened after the character's change in attitude towards politicians?**

A He avoided people with whom he had previously been friendly.
B He tried not to let it affect his attitude towards other people.
C He felt a need not to let it influence his children.
D He began to support a different kind of politician.

4

The limitations of selfishness

The rational-actor model of economics assumes that people are selfish in the narrow sense. It says that the world is bitterly competitive, and that those who do not pursue their own interests ruthlessly are likely to be swept aside by others who do.

It is true that self-interest is an important human motive, and the self-interest model does effectively explain much typical human behaviour. When energy prices rise, for example, people are more likely to buy vehicles that are more fuel efficient and add extra insulation to their attics. But some economists argue that self-interest explains virtually all behaviour. As Gordon Tullock of the University of Arizona has written, for example, 'the average human being is about 95 per cent selfish in the narrow sense of the term.'

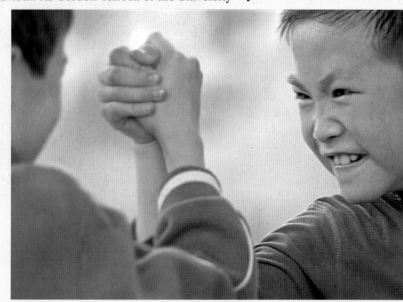

Is he right? Or do we often heed social and cultural norms that urge us to set aside self-interest in the name of some greater good? For example, people make anonymous donations to charity or public organizations. From society's perspective, our willingness to reject self-interest in such instances leads to better outcomes than when we all act in a purely selfish manner.

My point is not that my fellow economists are wrong to emphasize the importance of self-interest. But those who insist that it is the only important human motive are missing something important. Even more troubling, the narrow self-interest model, which encourages us to expect the worst in others, often encourages the worst in us as well.

5   The writer uses the purchase of vehicles and donations to charity as examples of

   A   his belief that only a minority of people are completely selfish.
   B   the way in which some people's attitudes are changing.
   C   his theory that the same person can be both selfish and unselfish.
   D   types of behaviour that may not seem logical.

5

6   The writer's view of the theory supported by other economists is that

   A   it can give people a justification for their selfish behaviour.
   B   it is not something that people recognize in themselves.
   C   it is more true of some people than of others.
   D   it is based on an incorrect starting point.

6

You are going to read a newspaper article about some creatures. Six paragraphs have been removed from the article. Choose from the paragraphs A–G the one which fits each gap (7–12). There is one extra paragraph which you do not need to use.

Mark your answers on the separate answer sheet.

Crocodile Science Reveals Secrets

To the casual observer, an adult alligator afloat in an algae-dappled pond, its two-meter body motionless except for the sporadic darting of its devilish amber eyes, might conjure up any number of images, none of them comforting. For Dr. Daphne Soares, however, a neuroscientist at the University of Maryland, an alligator looks like nothing so much as a big, amphibious and grievously misunderstood kitten.

7

'But I absolutely love these creatures,' she said. 'They're beautiful, elegant and goofy at the same time.' They are also unmistakeably observant and curious. She said they have a bad reputation for 'being stupid little reptiles.' But she added, 'They're very curious, very alert, and they want to know what's going on.' Dr Soares has worked with many species of Crocodylia, the reptilian order that includes crocodiles, alligators, caimans and gharials. And while she admires the entire crocodilian dynasty, alligators are her favorite.

Dr Soares specializes in neuroethology – the neural underpinnings of animal behavior – and has recently discovered a kind of sixth sense unique to crocodilians, which are often referred to generically as crocodiles. She has determined that the mysterious little bumps found around the jaws of some crocodile species and across the entire bodies of others, which naturalists had long observed but never before understood, are sensory organs exquisitely suited to the demands of a semi-submerged ambush predator.

8

The discovery of this novel sensory system is just one of a number of new findings about the prowess and performance of crocodilians, which have survived for 230 million years, some by land, others by sea, most astraddle. 'Our primate ancestors were ratty little things that went around stealing eggs,' said Dr. Perran Ross, a crocodile specialist and professor of wildlife ecology and conservation at the University of Florida. 'Ancestral crocodiles had basically the same body plan we see today, apparently because it works.'

9

'This means that crocodiles have tremendous robustness against bacterial infection,' Dr. Ross said. 'The sort of wound that would leave any of us severely septicemic doesn't seem to touch them.' That capability has inspired researchers to begin screening crocodile blood in search of new antibiotics.

10

'They're not like big lizards,' said Dr. George Amato, a geneticist at the World Conservation Society, a division of the Bronx Zoo in New York. 'It's clear when you spend time with them that they're quite complex.'

They're not always like one another, either. Dr. Amato and his colleagues, including Dr. John Thorbjarnarson of the conservation society in Florida, are close to declaring that the so-called Nile crocodile, the giant meat-eater renowned throughout Africa for having the might to prey on adult zebras and the occasional fisherman, may not be a single species of crocodile, as has long been thought.

11

Since there are only about two dozen crocodilian species in the world today, a new family herald would be considered a major event in the annals of crocodilian research. It would probably take years for it to gain general acceptance and appropriate nomenclature.

12

'Crocodiles,' Dr. Thorbjarnarson said, 'really are the closest things we have to living examples of those creatures from the distant past.'

A   This is borne out by the facts. The 23 species of the order Crocodylia include alligators, crocodiles, caimans and gharials. Crocodiles tend to have narrow, V-shaped snouts, while alligators' jaws are rounder. Also, a crocodile's lower teeth are visible when its mouth is closed.

B   As scientists are just beginning to appreciate, that physical structure is like an armored tank. Beneath the scaly sheath and craggy osteoderms is another layer of armor, built of rows of overlapping shingles, or osteoscutes, that are both strong and flexible. And beneath that formidable barrier is an equally formidable immune system.

C   Crocodiles are an impressively ancient and resilient clan. They hark back to a cast of beloved goliaths, called dinosaurs. The resemblance is not circumstantial. Through recent taxonomic analysis, scientists have concluded that dinosaurs, crocodiles and birds should be classified together on one branch of the great polylimbed Sequoia of Life.

D   Rather, there may be two distinct types, one in East Africa and Madagascar, the other adding excitement to the rivers and watering holes of Central and West Africa. The two populations look roughly the same, yet the DNA sequences of the two crocodile factions are so distinct that they may not even be each other's closest relatives.

E   Sure, they have thick scales and bulging bony knobs called osteoderms rather than fur. And yes, they have 80 teeth to the house cat's 30, and a tail that can dislocate your jaw with a single whack.

F   Crocodilians are also thinking creatures, and will engage in sophisticated behavior uncommon to most reptiles. They vocalize to each other. They squabble over status and can distinguish between a friendly hominid and a pest. In caring for their young, they are more protective than a mother hen, for what hen can keep her babies from harm by carrying them in her jaw?

G   These pigmented nodules encase bundles of nerve fibers that respond to the slightest disturbance in surface water and thus allow a crocodile to detect the signature of a potential meal – an approaching fish, a bathing heron, a luckless fawn enjoying its last lick of water.

You are going to read an extract from a novel. For questions 13–19, choose the answer (A, B, C or D) which you think fits best according to the text.

Mark your answers on the separate answer sheet.

Thirty or so years after he arrived in London, Chanu decided that it was time to see the sights. 'All I saw was the Houses of Parliament. And that was in 1979.' It was a project. Much equipment was needed. Preparations were made. Chanu bought a pair of shorts which hung just below his knees. He tried them on and filled the numerous pockets with a compass, guidebook, binoculars, bottled water, maps and two types of disposable camera. Thus loaded, the shorts hung at mid-calf. He bought a baseball cap and wore it around the flat with the visor variously angled up and down and turned around to the back of his head. A money belt secured the shorts around his waist and prevented them from reaching his ankles. He made a list of tourist attractions and devised a star rating system that encompassed historical significance, something he termed 'entertainment factor' and value for money. The girls would enjoy themselves. They were forewarned of this requirement.

On a hot Saturday morning towards the end of July the planning came to fruition. 'I've spent more than half my life here,' said Chanu, 'but I've hardly left these few streets.' He stared out of the bus windows at the grimy colours of Bethnal Green Road. 'All this time I have been struggling and struggling, and I've barely had time to lift my head and look around.'

They sat at the front of the bus, on the top deck. Chanu shared a seat with Nazneen, and Shahana and Bibi sat across the aisle. Nazneen crossed her ankles and tucked her feet beneath the seat to make way for the two plastic carrier bags that contained their picnic. 'You'll stink the bus out,' Shahana had said. 'I'm not sitting with you.' But she had not moved away.

'It's like this,' said Chanu, 'when you have all the time in the world to see something, you don't bother to see it. Now that we are going home, I have become a tourist.' He pulled his sunglasses from his forehead onto his nose. They were part of the new equipment.

He turned to the girls. 'How do you like your holiday so far?' Bibi said that she liked it very well, and Shahana squinted and shuffled and leaned her head against the side window.

Chanu began to hum. He danced with his head, which wobbled from side to side, and drummed out a rhythm on his thigh. The humming appeared to come from low down in his chest and melded with the general tune of the bus, vibrating on the bass notes.

Nazneen decided that she would make this day unlike any other. She would not allow this day to disappoint him.

The conductor came to collect fares. He had a slack-jawed expression: nothing could interest him. 'Two at one pound, and two children, please,' said Chanu. He received his tickets. 'Sightseeing,' he announced, and flourished his guidebook. 'Family holiday.'

'Right,' said the conductor. He jingled his bag, looking for change. He was squashed by his job. The ceiling forced him to stoop.

'Can you tell me something? To your mind, does the British Museum rate more highly than the National Gallery? Or would you recommend the gallery over the museum?'

The conductor pushed his lower lip out with his tongue. He stared hard at Chanu, as if considering whether to eject him from the bus.

'In my rating system,' explained Chanu, 'they are neck and neck. It would be good to take an opinion from a local.'

'Where've you come from, mate?'

'Oh, just two blocks behind,' said Chanu. 'But this is the first holiday for twenty or thirty years.'

The conductor swayed. It was still early but the bus was hot and Nazneen could smell his sweat. He looked at Chanu's guidebook. He twisted round and looked at the girls. At a half-glance he knew everything about Nazneen, and then he shook his head and walked away.

13 In what sense was the sightseeing trip a 'project' (line 4)?

  A Chanu felt a duty to do it.
  B It was something that Chanu had wanted to do for a long time.
  C Chanu took it very seriously.
  D It was something that required a good deal of organization.

14 The descriptions of Chanu's clothing are intended to

  A show how little he cared about his appearance.
  B create an impression of his sense of humour.
  C create amusing visual images of him.
  D show how bad his choice of clothes always was.

15 Chanu had decided to go on a sightseeing trip that day because

  A he regretted the lack of opportunity to do so before.
  B he felt that it was something the girls ought to do.
  C he had just developed an interest in seeing the sights.
  D he had grown bored with the area that he lived in.

16 As they sat on top of the bus,

  A Nazneen began to regret bringing so much food with them.
  B the girls felt obliged to pretend that they were enjoying themselves.
  C Chanu explained why he had brought the whole family on the trip.
  D the family members showed different amounts of enthusiasm for the trip.

17 When Chanu showed him the guidebook, the conductor

  A made it clear that he wanted to keep moving through the bus.
  B appeared to think that Chanu might cause a problem.
  C initially pretended not to have heard what Chanu said.
  D felt that he must have misunderstood what Chanu said.

18 What was strange about Chanu's use of the word 'local'?

  A It was not relevant to the places he was asking about.
  B It could equally have been applied to him.
  C He was not using it with its normal meaning.
  D He had no reason to believe it applied to the conductor.

19 What do we learn about the trip from the text as a whole?

  A Chanu regarded it as a kind of holiday.
  B Nazneen could not see the point of doing it.
  C It was typical of the kind of thing that Chanu often did.
  D The family's attitude to it changed once it had started.

PART 4

You are going to read an article about various paintings. For questions 20–34, choose from the paintings (A–D). The paintings may be chosen more than once.

Mark your answers on the separate answer sheet.

Of which painting are the following stated?

It was considered not to be typical of paintings produced from certain sources.	20
The artist likes to depict events and situations that are open to different interpretations.	21
It is of something that no longer exists.	22
The artist points out that it is based on things actually observed, even though it doesn't depict them accurately.	23
The artist specializes in things that most people regard as ugly.	24
A deduction that could be made about what is happening in it is not what the artist is actually showing.	25
The artist took a risk while creating it.	26
The artist denies that there was a particular influence on its style.	27
The artist checks that nothing important is missing from preparatory work.	28
Its success suggests a change of attitude on the part of the judges.	29
It was completely altered in order to produce various connections.	30
The artist always tries to portray certain unique characteristics.	31
Its artist produces paintings in different locations.	32
In one way, it is unlike any other painting the artist has produced.	33
The artist likes to find by chance subjects that have certain characteristics.	34

Watercolour competition

THE WINNERS

First prize

A Carol Robertson *Interrupted Field*

This unique competition is now in its 19th year, and for much of that time you might be forgiven for thinking that the judges weren't halfway bold enough. In the beginning, the selection of an abstract painting for the exhibition, let alone as a prize-winner, would have been totally unexpected. Though changes began to occur some years ago, an abstract painting has never won first prize. Until now.

Carol Robertson's Interrupted Field is a worthy winner, a more or less geometric composition that exploits the qualities of evenly-applied washes of colour. The painting is vast – 'the largest I've ever attempted' – so the big, even area of blue in the centre is, apart from anything else, something of a technical achievement.

Robertson is keen to stress that her abstract compositions are firmly rooted in reality. Though she doesn't 'seek to confirm or record the way the world looks', her work is never disconnected from the natural world, so the coloured stripes and bands in this painting

have a specific source. Over the past five years, Robertson has been working in Ireland, on the northwest coast of County Mayo. The coloured stripes stimulate 'memories of coastal landscape, brightly painted cottages, harbours and fishing boats, things seen out of the corner of my eye as I explored that coastline by car and on foot. The colour mirrors the fragments of life that caught my eye against a background of sea and sky.'

Runners up

B Geoffrey Wynne *Quayside*

Geoffrey Wynne describes himself as 'an open-air impressionist watercolour painter', though he adds that 'larger works', this prize-winning picture among them, 'are developed in the studio'. It struck the judges as something of a tour de force, a complex composition in which most of the detail had to be suppressed in order to preserve a sense of pictorial unity. It also has a vividness and directness not usually associated with paintings worked up from sketches and photographs.

Perhaps the most noteworthy aspect of this painting is the sheer number of people in it. According to the title, they are on a quay somewhere, and the number of suitcases they have with them suggests they have just landed from a boat on the first stage of a holiday. 'Yes, that's almost right,' Wynne told me, 'except that we're on the boat in the early morning, just arrived back from Mallorca, and the people are waiting to get on. This painting took a long time to finish, and many earlier attempts were abandoned. To achieve a unity, I immersed the half-finished painting in the bath, then added the black with a big brush. It's dangerous to do, because you can't really control the effects. Then I reworked everything, establishing links with colour and tone throughout the composition, creating a kind of web or net of similar effects.'

C Arthur Lockwood *Carbonizer Tower*

There were other, less prosaic titles among the thousand-or-so entries to this year's competition, but there were few more fetching paintings – or, come to that, more experienced painters in watercolour. Arthur Lockwood has a big reputation among watercolour painters and watercolour enthusiasts, chiefly for his accomplished pictures of industrial sites, subjects that are generally thought to be unsightly, but have striking visual qualities all their own. Among them is a kind of romanticism stimulated by indications of decay and the passing of irrecoverable time. Lockwood's subjects are, after all, ruins, the modern equivalent of Gothic churches overgrown by ivy. He aims not only to reveal those qualities, but to make a visual record of places that are fast being destroyed. This painting, a good example of his work in general, is one of an extensive series on the same subject. What we see is part of a large industrial plant that once made smokeless coal briquettes. It has now been closed and demolished to make way for a business park.

D Michael Smee *Respite at The Royal Oak*

Michael Smee was once a successful stage and television designer. This is worth stressing, because this prize-winning painting makes a strong theatrical impression. Smee agrees, and thinks it has much to do with the carefully judged lighting. 'As a theatre designer, you make the set, which comes to life only when it's lit.' The obvious affinity with Edward Hopper's work is 'just a coincidence', Smee says. 'The other picture I submitted isn't at all like Hopper.' Both artists, though, share an interest in suggesting ambiguous narratives.

Smee prefers to happen on pubs and cafés that are intriguing visually and look as though they might be under threat. He has a strong desire to record 'not only the disappearing pub culture peculiar to this country, but also bespoke bar interiors and the individuals therein'. He works his paintings up from informative sketches. 'I get there early, before many people have arrived, sit in the corner and scribble away. Then, once the painting is in progress in the studio, I make a return visit to reassure myself and to note down what I'd previously overlooked.' His main aim isn't topographical accuracy, however; it's to capture the appearance of artificial and natural light together, as well as the reflections they make.

Paper 2: Writing (1 hour 30 minutes)

PART 1

You **must** answer this question. Write your answer in 180–220 words in an appropriate style.

1 As a member of the entertainments committee at the place where you work or study, you have been asked to write a report on the events that the committee organized over the past year. Read the advertisements for the events and the notes you made after the events. Then, using the information appropriately, write your report for the committee.

THEATRE TRIP TUESDAY 19TH MARCH

'THE MISUNDERSTANDING'
A NEW COMEDY AT THE BRIDGE THEATRE.

'The funniest comedy for ages'
according to the local paper's film critic.

Travel to theatre and back by coach.

CONTACT **MIKE** FOR TICKETS

Music Evening Friday 20th June, Main Hall

Come and see the best local bands
All kinds of music from jazz to rap

Tickets from Zoe - get them now, they'll sell out quickly!

ANNUAL PARTY
SATURDAY 1ST AUGUST, MAIN HALL

A great chance to meet new people

Wonderful food

NO NEED TO BOOK - SIMPLY TURN UP!

Theatre Trip: play great, v funny, but not many came; coach expensive, lost money on event; more advertising needed if we do it again

Music Evening: great success; lots of v talented local bands to choose from; great atmosphere, enjoyed by all; tickets sold out, made big profit

Annual Party: too many people, v crowded; sell tickets in future; food much enjoyed, v varied, made small profit

Write your **report**. You should use your own words as far as possible.

PART 2

Write an answer to one of the questions 2–5 in this part. Write your answer in 220–260 words in an appropriate style.

2 You have seen this announcement in an international magazine.

> **ARTICLES INVITED**
> --
> As part of a special section on modern inventions, we're looking for articles from readers about what they'd like to be invented in the future. What invention or inventions would you most like someone to come up with, and why? Give us all the details and tell us why these things would be useful to you, or to people in general. Send your articles to the address below.

Write your article.

3 You see the following announcement in an international magazine.

> **LIVE PERFORMANCE REVIEWS WANTED**
>
> Have you seen someone perform live who you had previously only heard on recordings or seen on TV or in films? We'd like you to send us reviews of concerts by bands you'd never seen live before or actors you'd never seen on stage. Describe the performance in detail. What did you think and what did the rest of the audience think? Compare the live performance with how the same person / people perform in recordings or on TV or in films. Were they not so good live, or did you prefer them live? Did your opinion of them change? Send your reviews to the address below.

Write your review.

4 Your teacher has asked you to write an essay on the following topic.

> Everyone should travel to other countries at some point in their lives because travel is an essential experience.

Write your essay.

5 Answer one of the following two questions based on your reading of one of the set books.

Either

5(a) Write a summary of the plot that includes he most important details and events and makes clear what the book is about and what happens in it.

Or

5(b) Write an essay about one or more characters that you sympathized with when you read the book and one or more characters who you disliked, giving reasons for your feelings about those characters.

Paper 3: Use of English (1 hour)

PART 1

For questions 1–12, read the text below and decide which answer (A, B, C or D) best fits each gap. There is an example at the beginning (0).

Mark your answers on the separate answer sheet.

Example:

0 **A** regarded   **B** said   **C** presented   **D** proposed

0	A	B	C	D

Thomas Cook

Thomas Cook could be 0 _____ to have invented the global tourist industry. He was born in England in 1808 and became a cabinet-maker. Then he 1 _____ on the idea of using the newly-invented railways for pleasure trips and by the summer of 1845, he was organizing commercial trips. The first was to Liverpool and 2 _____ a 60-page handbook for the journey, the 3 _____ of the modern holiday brochure.

The Paris Exhibition of 1855 4 _____ him to create his first great tour, taking in France, Belgium and Germany. This also included a remarkable 5 _____ – Cook's first cruise, an extraordinary journey along the Rhine. Nothing like this had been available before, but it was only the beginning. Cook had invented 6 _____ tourism and now became a pioneering giant, striding across the world, travelling incessantly, researching every little detail before being absolutely confident that he could send the public to 7 _____ his steps.

Cook was not slow in thinking beyond Europe, and he turned his gaze upon Africa. The expertise he had gained with his pioneering cruise along the Rhine in 1855 8 _____ him in good stead when it came to organizing a fantastic journey along the Nile in 1869. Few civilians had so much as 9 _____ foot in Egypt, let 10 _____ travelled along this waterway through history and the remains of a vanished civilization 11 _____ back thousands of years. Then, in 1872, Cook organized, and took part in, the first conducted world tour. The whole adventure took 222 days and the 12 _____ of travel has not been the same since.

1	**A** dawned	**B** struck	**C** hit	**D** crossed
2	**A** featured	**B** presented	**C** inserted	**D** highlighted
3	**A** pioneer	**B** forerunner	**C** prior	**D** foretaste
4	**A** livened	**B** initiated	**C** launched	**D** inspired
5	**A** breakthrough	**B** leap	**C** step	**D** headway
6	**A** common	**B** whole	**C** wide	**D** mass
7	**A** retreat	**B** retrace	**C** resume	**D** retrieve
8	**A** kept	**B** took	**C** stood	**D** made
9	**A** set	**B** placed	**C** laid	**D** put
10	**A** apart	**B** aside	**C** alone	**D** away
11	**A** flowing	**B** going	**C** running	**D** passing
12	**A** scene	**B** area	**C** land	**D** world

For questions 13–27, read the text below and think of the word which best fits each gap. Use only one word in each gap. There is an example at the beginning (0).

Write your answers IN CAPITAL LETTERS on the separate answer sheet.

Example:

0	W	O	U	L	D							

Cyber history for sale

In the spring of 1946, J. Presper Eckert and John Maunchly sent out a business plan for a company that **0** _____ sell 'electronic computers'. In their eight-page proposal for **13** _____ financing of this enterprise, sent to a small group of prospective backers, the two engineers predicted that the market for **14** _____ a machine might consist **15** _____ scientific laboratories, universities and government agencies. Such **16** _____ the beginnings of the Electronic Control Company of Philadelphia, which produced the Univac, the first computer **17** _____ be commercially sold in the United States.

Recently, Christie's in New York auctioned the original typescript of the Eckert-Maunchly proposal **18** _____ $72,000 to a private buyer. It was sold **19** _____ part of a collection called 'The Origins of Cyberspace', which contained about 1,000 books, papers, brochures and **20** _____ artefacts from the history of computing.

'It's becoming the new frontier in scientific collecting,' said Thomas Lecky, who **21** _____ charge of the auction. Mr Lecky said two items **22** _____ particular had generated interest among prospective bidders. **23** _____ were the Eckert-Maunchly business plan and a technical journal containing the idea for TCP / IP, the standard system for the transmission of information over the Internet. **24** _____ someone approached him 10 years ago with the May 1974 issue of the engineering journal in **25** _____ the TCP / IP paper appeared, he would have thought that it would have been of absolutely **26** _____ interest to anyone. 'You don't really know when history is **27** _____ made,' he said.

For questions 28–37, read the text below. Use the word given in capitals at the end of some of the lines to form a word that fits in the gap in the same line. There is an example at the beginning (0).

Write your answers IN CAPITAL LETTERS on the separate answer sheet.

Example:

| 0 | O | P | E | R | A | T | I | O | N | | | |

CITICAR

What is CitiCar?

CitiCar is an 0 _____ that provides cars for rent by the   OPERATE

hour, day, week or month from an ever-expanding 28 _____ of   NET

reserved spaces in several UK cities. Our brand new cars can be booked

for any 29 _____ of time from as little as one hour to six months   LONG

and can be collected or returned at your 30 _____ 24 hours a day,   CONVENIENT

seven days a week.

Greener CitiCar

Car sharing is 31 _____ to the urban environment. On average, each   BENEFIT

CitiCar takes five privately owned cars off the road because our members

often sell a car when they join. This means we've already taken over 450

cars off the UK's crowded roads, 32 _____ congestion and freeing up   EASY

parking spaces. Our research has shown that people drive 59%

fewer miles when they join us. This means we will prevent the 33 _____   EMIT

of nearly 1,000,000 kg of CO_2 over the next couple of years!

Business CitiCar

CitiCar can save your business time, trouble and money. We work in

34 _____ with organizations of all sizes and types, allowing them to   PARTNER

supplement or 35 _____ their fleets of cars and to improve their   PLACE

36 _____. We also work with hotels, business centres and property   EFFICIENT

37 _____, helping them attract more clients by offering a shared car   DEVELOP

car scheme as part of their portfolio.

PART 4

For questions 38–42, think of one word only which can be used appropriately in all three sentences. Here is an example (0).

Example:

0   If you're _____ next weekend, perhaps we could get together then.

This seat is _____ if you want to sit on it.

Feel _____ to stay with us any time you need a place to stay.

Example:

| 0 | F | R | E | E | | | | | | | | | |

Write only the missing word IN CAPITAL LETTERS *on the separate answer sheet.*

---

38 Are you completely _____ as to what you have to do now?

The sound isn't very _____ – I think there must be a problem with the speakers.

The sky was _____ and there wasn't a cloud in sight.

39 I can't _____ why it's necessary for us to do this immediately.

Many people _____ money as the most important thing in life.

I demanded to _____ the manager to discuss my complaint.

40 When he's not working, George's main _____ is music, particularly jazz..

Politics is of no _____ to Suzanne and she knows nothing about it.

We had to pay a very high rate of _____ on the loan from the bank.

41 I've got a _____ reason for being so angry and I'll explain it to you.

You need a _____ level of English for that job.

People were _____ to me in every place I visited and helped me a lot.

42 I'm not going to _____ the whole story, I'll just sum up what happened.

The series is very popular because viewers can _____ to the main characters in it.

The examples given here don't _____ to my personal experience.

For questions 43–50, complete the second sentence so that it has a similar meaning to the first sentence, using the word given. Do not change the word given. You must use between three and six words, including the word given. Here is an example (0).

Example:

0   I didn't know the way there, so I got lost.

GET

Not _____ there, I got lost.

0	K	N	O	W	I	N	G		H	O	W		T	O		G	E	T

Write the missing words IN CAPITAL LETTERS *on the separate answer sheet.*

43   I've been too busy to answer my emails, but I'll do it soon.

ROUND

I _____ my emails yet, but I'll do it soon.

44   This computer is useless to me, so you can have it.

USE

This computer is _____ to me, so you can have it.

45   It's nearly lunchtime, so would you like to eat something?

FEEL

It's nearly lunchtime, so _____ to eat?

46   The ambulance came within minutes.

MATTER

It _____ before the ambulance came.

47   Experts say that things are bound to improve.

DOUBT

Experts say that there is _____ better.

48   Jake was the person who started my interest in collecting pottery.

GOT

It _____ in collecting pottery.

49   He really wanted to impress the interviewers.

DESPERATE

He _____ the interviewers a good impression.

50   Because he was injured he couldn't play in the next game.

PREVENTED

His _____ in the next game.

Paper 4: Listening (40 minutes)

You will hear three different extracts. For questions 1–6, choose the answer (A, B or C) which fits best according to what you hear. There are two questions for each extract.

Extract One

You hear two people talking about reading books aloud for children.

1 The second speaker says that she believes that
- A her children enjoy listening to her read aloud.
- B she shares a reading habit with other parents.
- C parents should read aloud to children.

| | 1 |

2 What do both speakers talk about?
- A their children's reactions when they read aloud to them
- B their selfish motives for reading aloud to their children
- C their dramatic approach to reading aloud to their children

| | 2 |

Extract Two

You hear part of a radio programme.

3 The presenter says that some people start businesses with friends because
- A they see other people doing it.
- B they don't trust outsiders.
- C they lack the courage to do it alone.

| | 3 |

4 What was Matt's attitude to his partner?
- A He felt their friendship was more important that the business.
- B He was angry that his partner didn't do his share of the work.
- C He thought that he had expected too much of his partner.

| | 4 |

Extract Three

You hear two people on a radio programme talking about running.

5 Who are the two speakers?
- A successful athletes
- B fitness experts
- C sports journalists

| | 5 |

6 Both speakers agree that, to improve as a runner, runners should
- A limit the amount of training they do.
- B develop their own personal training methods.
- C vary the focus of their training.

| | 6 |

You will hear someone who works as a life coach talking about her work.
For questions 7–14, complete the sentences.

BEING A LIFE COACH

The speaker tells people who ask her that her work is connected with the

[7] .

The speaker says that most people concentrate too much on what she calls their

' [8] '.

The speaker calls the plan to achieve a specific goal a ' [9] '.

The speaker gives as an example of a personal goal increasing your ability at

[10] .

The speaker gives as an example of a business goal thinking of new

[11] .

The speaker says that sessions are conducted in a way that prevents any

[12] .

The speaker says that sessions do not involve dealing with a person's

[13] .

The speaker says that life coaches enable people to become [14]

themselves.

You will hear a radio discussion about children who invent imaginary friends. For questions 15–20, choose the answer (A, B, C or D) which fits best according to what you hear.

15 In the incident that Liz describes,
   A her daughter asked her to stop the car.
   B she had to interrupt the journey twice.
   C she got angry with her daughter.
   D her daughter wanted to get out of the car.

   `15`

16 What does the presenter say about the latest research into imaginary friends?
   A It contradicts other research on the subject.
   B It shows that the number of children who have them is increasing.
   C It indicates that negative attitudes towards them are wrong.
   D It focuses on the effect they have on parents.

   `16`

17 How did Liz feel when her daughter had an imaginary friend?
   A always confident that it was only a temporary situation
   B occasionally worried about the friend's importance to her daughter
   C slightly confused as to how she should respond sometimes
   D highly impressed by her daughter's inventiveness

   `17`

18 Karen says that one reason why children have imaginary friends is that
   A they are having serious problems with their real friends.
   B they can tell imaginary friends what to do.
   C they want something that they cannot be given.
   D they want something that other children haven't got.

   `18`

19 Karen says that the teenager who had invented a superhero is an example of
   A a very untypical teenager.
   B a problem that imaginary friends can cause.
   C something she had not expected to discover.
   D how children change as they get older.

   `19`

20 According to Karen, how should parents react to imaginary friends?
   A They should pretend that they like the imaginary friend.
   B They shouldn't get involved in the child's relationship with the friend.
   C They should take action if the situation becomes annoying.
   D They shouldn't discuss the imaginary friend with their child.

   `20`

PART 4

You will hear five short extracts in which people are talking about the music industry.

Task one

For questions 21–25, choose from the list A–H who is speaking.

While you listen you must complete both tasks.

A a recording studio engineer

B a musician

C a reviewer

D a club owner

E a fan

F a website operator

G a manager of performers

H a radio presenter

Speaker 1 [ ] 21

Speaker 2 [ ] 22

Speaker 3 [ ] 23

Speaker 4 [ ] 24

Speaker 5 [ ] 25

Task two

For questions 26–30, choose from the list A–H the opinion each speaker expresses.

A Tastes in music change very quickly.

B Music is an important part of culture.

C Some people who become well-known don't deserve their success.

D There are lots of dishonest people in the music business.

E Artists need to have a realistic view of the music business.

F People with real talent will always succeed.

G Some artists will always be popular.

H People should only get involved in music because they love it.

Speaker 1 [ ] 26

Speaker 2 [ ] 27

Speaker 3 [ ] 28

Speaker 4 [ ] 29

Speaker 5 [ ] 30

Paper 5: Speaking (15 minutes)

PART 1 (3 minutes)

Aims and ambitions

- What are your aims and ambitions for the future?
- What will you have to do to achieve those aims and ambitions?
- Do you think you will achieve your aims and ambitions? ..... (Why? / Why not?)
- What aims and ambitions do other people from your country have? ..... (Why?)
- What do you consider to be success in life? ..... (Why?)

Social life

- What kind of things do you do with your friends?
- Would you say that you have an exciting social life? ..... (Why? / Why not?)
- Do you like parties? If so, what kind of parties do you like most? If not, why not?
- What aspect of your social life do you enjoy most? ..... (Why?)
- Has your social life changed over the years? If so, how? If not, why not?

PART 2 (4 minutes)

1 Running
2 Speaking in public

Candidate A	Look at the three photographs 1A, 1B and 1C on page 134. They show people running. Compare two of the photographs and say why the people might be running, and what kind of lives they may have. *Candidate A talks on his/her own for about 1 minute.*
Candidate B	Which of the pictures is closest to something you have done or experienced, and why? *Candidate B talks on his/her own for about 20 seconds.*
Candidate B	Look at the three photographs 2A, 2B and 2C on page 134. They show people speaking in public. Compare two of the photographs and say **what the people might be talking about, and what the situation might be.** *Candidate B talks on his/her own for about 1 minute.*
Candidate A	Which of the speakers would you prefer to listen to, and why? *Candidate A talks on his/her own for about 20 seconds.*

PARTS 3 AND 4 (8 minutes)

Environmental issues

PART 3

Look at the pictures on page 135 showing different environmental issues.

First, talk to each other about which environmental issue each picture shows and how serious each problem is. Then decide which picture(s) show(s) a problem that is being solved or can most easily be solved, and discuss how it is being solved or can be solved.

Candidates A and B discuss this together for about 3 minutes.

PART 4

- Some people say that the environment is the biggest issue in the modern world. Do you agree? Do you think there are more important issues?
- What impact can individuals have concerning environmental issues? What do you do personally that is connected with environmental issues?
- Do you think that people in general are concerned about the environment? If so, what concerns them most? If not, why not?
- Many companies today advertise the ways in which they are environmentally-friendly. Is this a positive development or does it have little effect?
- What should governments be doing about environmental problems?

Paper 1: Reading (1 hour 15 minutes)

PART 1

You are going to read three extracts which are all concerned in some way with the mind. For questions 1–6, choose the answer (A, B, C or D) which you think fits best according to the text.

Mark your answers on the separate answer sheet.

Decisions, decisions

Scientists have discovered that the best way to make a decision is to collect the information you need, forget about it, and then trust your instincts to get it right. This advice comes from a study by researchers at the University of Amsterdam that focused on how people make shopping decisions and what kinds of strategies produce the best buys.

Decisions can be grouped into two basic categories: complex decisions, such as buying a house or a car, and simple decisions, such as choosing a shampoo. Most people would agonize over the former and scarcely think about the latter, which is precisely the wrong way to do it, according to Professor Ap Dijksterhuis and his colleagues. After a series of shopping experiments, they conclude that thinking really hard about a decision works well when the decision is simple. But when the decision gets more complicated, focusing all your attention on what to buy isn't usually the best approach.

Participants in the experiments were asked to choose between four different cars, and were given details of 12 attributes, including leg room and mileage, about each make and model. The scientists found that people identified the best car around 25 per cent of the time, which was no better than chance. The surprise came when the researchers distracted the participants with puzzles before asking them to make their choices. More than half then managed to pick the best car. Professor Dijksterhuis said: 'Your brain is capable of juggling lots of facts and possibilities at the same time when you let it work without specifically thinking about the decision. But when you are specifically thinking about a problem, your brain isn't able to weigh up as much information.'

1 Which of the following did the study conclude?
   A It is best not to concentrate on the issue when making a difficult decision.
   B It is not a good idea to put a lot of thought into a simple decision.
   C The first decision that people make is frequently the best one.
   D People tend to focus on irrelevant issues when making difficult decisions.

   [1]

2 Which of the following is true of the experiments?
   A The subjects showed that they did not like being distracted while they were thinking.
   B The researchers had decided beforehand what the correct choices were.
   C The researchers encouraged the subjects to stop thinking for a time.
   D The subjects were made aware of how appropriate their first decision had been.

   [2]

Musician can taste differences when she hears notes

Most musicians have to work hard to learn to identify musical intervals – two notes of a scale played at the same time. But a musician described in the current issue of *Nature* can actually taste some intervals, and some taste better than others.

Synaesthesia, a puzzling sensory phenomenon in which a sound evokes an experience of colour (the sound of a truck 'looks green') or a sight evokes a sound (a light coming on 'sounds like a bell') is well known, though rare. Even rarer are synaesthesias that involve taste or smell, phenomena that occur when someone can 'taste' a name, for example, or 'smell' a spoken word. But probably rarest of all, and according to the authors unique in the published literature, is the case of flavoured tone intervals in a professional musician.

Identifying tone intervals – the distance between two pitches – is a complex task that normally requires considerable formal musical training. But this woman, a 27-year-old professional musician identified only by the initials E.S. in the paper, consistently and inevitably experiences particular tastes when she hears specific musical intervals. Sometimes the flavour that E.S. tastes seems logical. A minor second (C and D flat played together) and a major seventh (C and B played together), which are mirror images of each other on the octave scale, both taste sour. A major second and a minor seventh, another mirror image pair, both taste bitter. She invariably finds that sounds that are pleasant to the ear also taste good, and unpleasant ones don't.

E.S. has had this ability since she was a child, but gave no conscious thought to it until she was about 16. In the beginning, when she realized this was something strange, she was a bit worried. But then she learned to use it, and now she likes it.

3 The writer says that the synaesthesia the musician experiences

   A involves a consistent pattern.
   B has changed in nature over a period of time.
   C involves more than one of the senses in addition to hearing.
   D does not occur at all with some tone intervals.

   [3]

4 Which of the following best describes the writer's tone when talking about the musician?

   A scepticism
   B amusement
   C amazement
   D sympathy

   [4]

SUCCESS: IT'S A BRAIN OF TWO HALVES

Knowledge is no longer power. A self-help book has become an unexpected hit with the prediction that success in the modern age will depend on the ability to tear up the rules and think laterally. The book, *A Whole New Mind*, argues that we need to develop the 'soft' skills in the right side of the brain. These, says the author, Daniel Pink, will eclipse the analytical ability controlled by the left side. The traditional knowledge-based professions – banking, law, management and engineering – will go the way of most blue-collar jobs, taken over by computers.

Pink's book has become a word-of-mouth success. In it, he says that as knowledge turns into a commodity owned by all, a flexible, unpredictable edge will become a necessary attribute for success. 'The first people who develop a whole mind will do extremely well,' said Pink. 'The rest, who move slowly or not at all, will suffer.'

Pink bases his arguments on analysis of the brain's capabilities, which has shown that while the left side analyses details in sequence, the right side sees the bigger picture at the same time. This means that the left side takes a leading role in processing text or speech, while the right handles more complex multi-faceted tasks such as interpreting facial expression and intonation.

Results from more than 2 million participants in the Myers-Briggs test used by employers to vet job applicants have shown that in both Britain and America, analytical types outnumber creative personalities. 'If you asked the first group to talk about an apple, they would give you the facts,' said Sebastien Bailey, a psychologist. 'They'd say, it's green, it grows on trees.' He said that the second group, better adapted to the challenges of the 21st century, would talk about other elements, such as the environment, or a Greek legend about awarding an apple to the most beautiful goddess. The best thinkers, said Bailey, can routinely switch between both ways of thinking.

---

5 Who does Daniel Pink mean by 'The rest' at the end of the second paragraph?

A everyone in traditional knowledge-based professions
B people whose knowledge is too narrow
C people whose strength is only in their use of the left side of the brain
D everyone who does not regard success as important

[5]

6 The example of talking about an apple is given in order to illustrate

A the difference between creative thinkers and analytical thinkers.
B how certain people can move from one way of thinking to another.
C the reason why creative thinkers are preferred to analytical thinkers.
D a type of question that employers are starting to ask in interviews.

[6]

You are going to read a magazine article about work. Six paragraphs have been removed from the article. Choose from the paragraphs A–G the one which fits each gap (7–12). There is one extra paragraph which you do not need to use.

Mark your answers on the separate answer sheet.

WHEN THE BOSS IS A BULLY

Every working adult has known one – a boss who loves making subordinates nervous, whose moods radiate through the office, sending workers scurrying, whose very voice causes stomach muscles to clench and pulses to quicken. In short, a boss who is a bully.

7

'It got to where I was twitching, literally, on the way to work,' said Carrie Clark, 52, a former teacher and school administrator in Sacramento, California, who said her boss of several years ago baited and insulted her for 10 months before she left the job. 'I had to take care of my health.'

8

Psychologists doing so as a result of studying the dynamics of groups and organizations are discovering why cruel bosses thrive. They are learning how employees make excuses for managers they despise and under what conditions workers are most likely to confront and expose a bullying employer.

9

But adult bullies in positions of power are already dominant, and they are just as likely to pick on a strong subordinate as a weak one, said Dr. Gary Namie, director of the Workplace Bullying and Trauma Institute, an advocacy group based in Bellingham, Washington. Women, Dr. Namie said, are at least as likely as men to be the aggressors, and they are more likely to be targets.

10

For example, a manager might use bullying to beat down a subordinate they regard as a threat to them, said Dr. Harvey A. Hornstein, a retired professor from Teachers College at Columbia University and the author of *Brutal Bosses and Their Prey*. Or a manager might be looking for a scapegoat to carry the department's, or the supervisor's, frustrations. But most often, Dr. Hornstein found, managers bullied subordinates for the sheer pleasure of exercising power. 'It was a kind of low-grade sadism that was the most common reason,' he said. 'They'd start on one person and then move on to someone else.'

11

Researchers find little relationship between people's attitudes toward their jobs and their productivity, as measured by the output and even the quality of their work. Even in the most hostile work environment, conscientious people keep doing the work they are paid for.

Management researchers do not know how effective it is to challenge a cruel boss directly because so few employees do it. One reason for this is that, for many people, clashes with a supervisor recall old conflicts with parents, siblings or other authority figures from childhood. Dr. Mark Levey, a psychotherapist in Chicago who consults with corporations, said that nasty bosses often elicited from subordinates defensive habits that they first developed as children, like reflexive submission. 'Once these defensive positions lock in,' Dr Levey said, 'it's like people are transported to a different reality and can no longer see what's actually happening to them and cannot adapt.'

12

So what can victims of a bullying boss do? One of the best strategies to manage a bullying employer, Dr. Hornstein has found in his research, is to watch for patterns in the tyrant's behavior. Maybe he is bad on Mondays, maybe a little better on Fridays. Maybe she is kinder before her lunch break than after. If some types of assignments spook the person more than others, avoid them, if possible.

A   Nevertheless, tyrants do spread misery, and from the outside it looks as if they are doing a fine job. It does not help matters, psychologists say, that people who enjoy abusing power frequently also revere it and are quick to offer that reverence to the even-more-powerful. Bullying bosses are often experts at bowing to their own superiors.

B   In leadership positions that require the exercise of sheer violent will – on the football field or the battlefield – this approach can be successful. But in an office or a factory, different rules apply, and bullying usually has more to do with the boss's personal feelings than with getting the job done.

C   The impact such a person has on the rest of the workforce is immense. Dissatisfaction spreads, rivalries simmer, sycophants flourish. Normally self-confident professionals dissolve into quivering bundles of neuroses.

D   Researchers have long been interested in the bullies of the playground, exploring what drives them and what effects they have on their victims. Only recently have investigators paid attention to the bullies of the workplace.

E   Another theory on this tendency to passive obedience is that subordinate status itself causes people to defer to a supervisor's judgment, especially in well-defined hierarchies. It's the boss's job to make decisions, and co-workers may think there is some legitimate hidden reason for the boss's behavior.

F   The mystifying thing about this pattern is that it does not appear to affect performance. Workers may loathe a bullying boss and hate going to work each morning, but they still perform.

G   Bullying bosses, studies find, differ in significant ways from the bullies of childhood. In the schoolyard, particularly among elementary school boys, bullies tend to victimize smaller or weaker children.

You are going to read a newspaper article about trees and leaves. For questions 13–19, choose the answer (A, B, C or D) which you think fits best according to the text.

Mark your answers on the separate answer sheet.

Those brilliant autumn leaves

As trees across the northern areas of the globe turn gold and crimson, scientists are debating exactly what these colours are for. The scientists do agree on one thing: the colours are for something. That represents a major shift in thinking. For decades, textbooks claimed that autumn colours were just a by-product of dying leaves. 'I had always assumed that autumn leaves were waste baskets,' said Dr. David Wilkinson, an evolutionary ecologist at Liverpool John Moores University in England. 'That's what I was told as a student.'

During spring and summer, leaves get their green cast from chlorophyll, the pigment that plays a major role in capturing sunlight. But the leaves also contain other pigments whose colours are masked during the growing season. In autumn, trees break down their chlorophyll and draw some of the components back into their tissues. Conventional wisdom regards autumn colours as the product of the remaining pigments, which are finally unmasked.

Evolutionary biologists and plant physiologists offer two different explanations for why natural selection has made autumn colours so widespread. Dr. William Hamilton, an evolutionary biologist at Oxford University, proposed that bright autumn leaves contain a message: they warn insects to leave them alone. Dr. Hamilton's 'leaf signal' hypothesis grew out of earlier work he had done on the extravagant plumage of birds. He proposed it served as an advertisement from males to females, indicating they had desirable genes. As females evolved a preference for those displays, males evolved more extravagant feathers as they competed for mates. In the case of trees, Dr. Hamilton proposed that the visual message was sent to insects. In the autumn, aphids and other insects choose trees where they will lay their eggs. When the eggs hatch the next spring, the larvae feed on the tree, often with devastating results. A tree can ward off these pests with poisons. Dr. Hamilton speculated that trees with strong defences might be able to protect themselves even further by letting egg-laying insects know what was in store for their eggs. By producing brilliant autumn colours, the trees advertised their lethality. As insects evolved to avoid the brightest leaves, natural selection favoured trees that could become even brighter.

'It was a beautiful idea,' said Marco Archetti, a former student of Dr. Hamilton who is now at the University of Fribourg in Switzerland. Dr. Hamilton had Mr. Archetti turn the hypothesis into a mathematical model. The model showed that warning signals could indeed drive the evolution of bright leaves – at least in theory. Another student, Sam Brown, tested the leaf-signal hypothesis against real data about trees and insects. 'It was a first stab to see what was out there,' said Dr. Brown, now an evolutionary biologist at the University of Texas.

The leaf-signal hypothesis has also drawn criticism, most recently from Dr. Wilkinson and Dr. H. Martin Schaefer, an evolutionary biologist at the University of Freiburg in Germany. Dr. Wilkinson and other critics point to a number of details about aphids and trees that do not fit Dr. Hamilton's hypothesis. Dr. William Hoch, a plant physiologist at the University of Wisconsin, argues that bright leaves appear on trees that have no insects to warn off. 'If you are up here in the north of Wisconsin, by the time the leaves change, all the insects that feed on foliage are gone,' Dr. Hoch said. In their article, Dr. Schaefer and Dr. Wilkinson argue that a much more plausible explanation for autumn colours can be found in the research of Dr. Hoch and other plant physiologists. Their recent work suggests that autumn colours serve mainly as a sunscreen.

Dr. Hamilton's former students argue that the leaf-signal hypothesis is still worth investigating. Dr. Brown believes that leaves might be able to protect themselves both from sunlight and from insects. Dr. Brown and Dr. Archetti also argue that supporters of the sunscreen hypothesis have yet to explain why some trees have bright colours and some do not. 'This is a basic question in evolution that they seem to ignore,' Dr. Archetti said. 'I don't think it's a huge concern,' Dr. Hoch replied. 'There's natural variation for every characteristic.'

Dr. Hamilton's students and their critics agree that the debate has been useful, because it has given them a deeper reverence for this time of year. 'People sometimes say that science makes the world less interesting and awesome by just explaining things away,' Dr. Wilkinson said. 'But with autumn leaves, the more you know about them, the more amazed you are.'

13 What is stated about the colours of autumn leaves in the first two paragraphs?

   A There has previously been no disagreement about what causes them.
   B The process that results in them has never been fully understood.
   C Different colours from those that were previously the norm have started to appear.
   D Debate about the purpose of them has gone on for a long time,

13

14 The writer says that Dr Hamilton's work has focused on

   A the different purposes of different colours.
   B the use of colour for opposite purposes.
   C the possibility that birds and insects have influenced each other's behaviour.
   D the increased survival rates of certain kinds of tree.

14

15 Dr Hamilton has suggested that there is a connection between

   A the colours of autumn leaves and the behaviour of insects.
   B the development of brighter leaves and the reduced numbers of certain types of insect.
   C the survival of trees and the proximity of insects to them.
   D the brightness of leaves and the development of other defence mechanisms in trees.

15

16 What is said about the work done by former students of Dr Hamilton?

   A Neither of them was able to achieve what they set out to do.
   B Mr Archetti felt some regret about the outcome of the work he did.
   C Both of them initiated the idea of doing the work.
   D Dr Brown did not expect to draw any firm conclusions from his work.

16

17 Critics of Dr Hamilton's theory have expressed the view that

   A it is impossible to generalize about the purpose of the colours of autumn leaves.
   B his theory is based on a misunderstanding about insect behaviour.
   C the colours of autumn leaves have a different protective function.
   D his theory can only be applied to certain kinds of insect.

17

18 In the debate between the two groups of people investigating the subject, it has been suggested that

   A something regarded as a key point by one side is in fact not important.
   B further research will prove that Dr Hamilton's theory is the correct one.
   C both sides may in fact be completely wrong.
   D the two sides should collaborate.

18

19 All the people involved in research on the subject of autumn leaves feel that

   A it highlights the mystery of the natural world.
   B it is one of the most complex areas they have ever investigated.
   C it concerns a phenomenon that ordinary people would like an explanation for.
   D it shows how interesting an area previously thought to be dull can be.

19

You are going to read an article about society in the US. For questions 20–34, choose from the sections of the article (A–E). The sections may be chosen more than once.

Mark your answers on the separate answer sheet.

In which section of the article are the following mentioned?

the fact that there is no single definition of the word 'class'	20
an opinion that is now regarded with disapproval by academics in general	21
a disadvantage that a certain attitude to life might have	22
an example of a success that was thought to be typical of what anyone could achieve	23
evidence that it used to be easier for people to move up in class than it is now	24
a belief that class divisions used to be much clearer than they are now	25
people who believe that each of the main classes is now divided into various groups	26
when detailed and reliable analysis of people changing from one class to another started	27
a belief that people do not always get what they deserve	28
an idea that makes people feel uneasy	29
an increase in the number of people who think that rising in class is related more to effort than to luck	30
a belief that class has become a more important issue rather than a less important one	31
the kinds of things that people who belong to the same class have in common	32
attempts to create situations in which there are no class divisions	33
a belief that a certain attitude to life is instinctive	34

Class in the United States

A A recent poll on class found that 40 per cent of Americans believe that the chance of moving up from one class to another had risen over the last 30 years, a period in which new research shows that it has not. Thirty-five per cent said that it had not changed, and only 23 per cent said that it had dropped. More Americans than 20 years ago believe it is possible to start out poor, work hard and become rich. They say hard work and a good education are more important to getting ahead than connections or a wealthy background. 'I think the system is as fair as you can make it,' said one respondent. 'I don't think life is necessarily fair. But if you persevere, you can overcome adversity. It has to do with a person's willingness to work hard, and I think it's always been that way.'

B One difficulty in talking about class is that the word means different things to different people. Class is rank, it is tribe, it is culture and taste. It is attitudes and assumptions, a source of identity, a system of exclusion. To some, it is just money or it is an accident of birth that can influence the outcome of a life. Some Americans barely notice it; others feel its weight in powerful ways. At its most basic, class is one way societies sort themselves out. Even societies built on the idea of eliminating class have had stark differences in rank. Classes are groups of people in similar economic and social position; people who, for that reason, may share political attitudes, lifestyles, consumption patterns, cultural interests and opportunities to get ahead.

C When societies were simpler, the class landscape was easier to read. Marx divided 19th-century societies into just two classes; Max Weber added a few more. As societies grew increasingly complex, the old classes became more heterogeneous. As some sociologists and marketing consultants see it, the commonly accepted big three – the upper, middle and working classes – have broken down into dozens of micro classes, defined by occupations or lifestyles. A few sociologists say that social complexity has made the concept of class meaningless. But many other researchers disagree. 'Class awareness and the class language is receding at the very moment that class has reorganized American society,' said Michael Hout, a professor of sociology at Berkeley. 'I find these "end of class" discussions naive and ironic, because we are at a time of booming inequality and this massive reorganization of where we live and how we feel, even in the dynamics of our politics. Yet people say, "Well, the era of class is over." '

D Many Americans say that they have moved up the class ladder. In the recent poll, 45 per cent of respondents said they were in a higher class than when they grew up, while just 16 per cent said they were in a lower one. Overall, 1 per cent described themselves as upper class, 15 per cent as upper middle class, 42 per cent as middle, 35 per cent as working and 7 per cent as lower. 'I grew up very poor and so did my husband,' said one respondent. 'We're not rich but we are comfortable; we are middle class and our son is better off than we are.' The original exemplar of American social mobility was almost certainly Benjamin Franklin, one of 17 children of a candle maker. About 20 years ago, when researchers first began to study mobility in a rigorous way, Franklin seemed representative of a truly fluid society, in which the rags-to-riches trajectory was the readily achievable ideal, just as the nation's self-image promised. But new studies of mobility, which methodically track people's earnings over decades, have found far less movement. Mobility happens, just not as rapidly as was once thought. 'We all know stories of poor families in which the next generation did much better,' said Gary Solon, a leading mobility researcher. 'But in the past, people would say, "Don't worry about inequality. The offspring of the poor have chances as good as the chances of the offspring of the rich." Well, that's not true. It's not respectable in scholarly circles any more to make that argument.'

E Americans have never been comfortable with the notion of a hierarchy based on anything other than talent and hard work. Class contradicts their assumptions about the American dream, equal opportunity and the reasons for their own successes and even failures. Americans, constitutionally optimistic, are disinclined to see themselves as stuck. Blind optimism has its pitfalls. If opportunity is taken for granted as something that will be there no matter what, then the country is less likely to do the hard work to make it happen. But defiant optimism has its strengths. Without confidence in the possibility of moving up, there would almost certainly be fewer success stories.

Paper 2: Writing (1 hour 30 minutes)

<u>PART 1</u>

You **must** answer this question. Write your answer in 180–220 *words in an appropriate style.*

1 A group of English-speaking visitors is going to come to the place where you work or study for a day next month. You have been asked to propose a programme for the day of their visit. Read the suggestions that were made at a recent meeting to discuss the subject and the notes you have made of your own ideas. Then, using the information appropriately, write your proposal for the visitors' programme.

Meeting 13 May
Suggestions for programme for overseas visitors (26 June)

- Welcome in reception area, short talk (by whom?)
- Tour of building (which parts? length of tour?)
- Talk on what we do here (given by? what aspects?)
- Lunch (attended by?)
- Talk on the city / local area (given by?)
- Give presents at end of day (which presents?)

Other ideas:

- *Split visitors up into small groups for tour*
- *Let them watch us doing what we do on a typical day*
- *Ask one or more of them to give a talk to us (about?)*
- *Question & Answer session (when?)*
- *Give them Information Pack (containing?)*
- *Organize an evening event as well (what?)*

Write your **proposal**. You should use your own words as far as possible.

PART 2

Write an answer to one *of the questions 2–5 in this part. Write your answer in* 220–260 *words in an appropriate style.*

2   You see this advertisement in an English-language magazine.

Festival Staff Required

We are looking for staff for an international rock festival, taking place over a three-day period in the west of England during the summer. We are looking for people with a good command of English who could work in the following areas:

- catering (food and drink stalls and tents)
- security (in the performance area, at entrances and around the site)
- first aid (for minor medical problems)
- retail (stalls selling merchandise relating to the artists appearing)

To apply, explain why you would like to work at the festival, give details of the role(s) you would prefer and why, and give reasons why you would be suitable. Send applications to the address below.

Write your letter of application.

3   As part of an international research project about education and work that you are involved in, you have been asked to write a contribution about what young people in your city, region or country do after they leave school. You have been told that your piece should include information about further studies that some young people do after they leave school and the kind of jobs that other young people do immediately after leaving school.

Write your research project contribution.

4   You see the following announcement about a competition in an international magazine.

Who would **YOU** like to spend a day with?

Which famous person would you most like to spend a day with? We're offering a box of goodies to the person who sends us the best entry. Why would you like to spend a day with that person?

What is it that you like about him/her? And what would you do on that day? Give details of how you and your chosen person would spend that day. Send your entries to the address below.

Write your competition entry.

5   Answer one of the following two questions based on your reading of one of the set books.
   Either

   5(a)   Write an essay describing the writer's style in the book. How does the writer try to achieve his/her aims in the book? What aspects of the writer's style do you think are particularly effective and which aspects are less effective?

   Or

   5(b)   Write the story of one or more of the characters before the book begins. What do you think the character(s) had done and what had happened to the character(s) before the start of the book?

Paper 3: Use of English (1 hour)

PART 1

For questions 1–12, read the text below and decide which answer (A, B, C or D) best fits each gap. There is an example at the beginning (0).

Mark your answers on the separate answer sheet.

Example:

0 **A** characterized   **B** indicated   **C** detailed   **D** accounted

0	**A**	**B**	**C**	**D**

High notes of the singing neanderthals

Neanderthals have been misunderstood. The early humanoids traditionally 0_____ as ape-like brutes were deeply emotional beings with high-pitched voices. They may 1_____ have sung to each other. This new image has 2_____ from two studies of the vocal apparatus and anatomy of the creatures that 3_____ Europe between 200,000 and 35,000 years ago.

The research shows that Neanderthal voices might 4_____ have produced loud, womanly and highly melodic sounds – not the roars and grunts previously 5_____ by most researchers. Stephen Mithen, Professor of Archaeology and author of one of the studies, said: 'What is emerging is a 6_____ of an intelligent and emotionally complex creature whose most likely 7_____ of communication would have been part language and part song.'

Mithen's work 8_____ with the first detailed study of a reconstructed Neanderthal skeleton. Anthropologists brought together bones and casts from several 9_____ to re-create the creature. The creature that emerges would have 10_____ markedly from humans. Neanderthals seem to have had an extremely powerful 11_____ and no waist. Professor Trenton Holliday believes they must have evolved their stocky body shapes to 12_____ heat when ice covered the world.

1	**A** further	**B** just	**C** even	**D** so
2	**A** revealed	**B** resulted	**C** concluded	**D** happened
3	**A** resided	**B** dwelt	**C** filled	**D** occupied
4	**A** likely	**B** truly	**C** well	**D** quite
5	**A** judged	**B** assumed	**C** considered	**D** taken
6	**A** picture	**B** sight	**C** spectacle	**D** design
7	**A** sort	**B** practice	**C** approach	**D** form
8	**A** coincides	**B** occurs	**C** relates	**D** co-operates
9	**A** grounds	**B** sites	**C** plots	**D** patches
10	**A** differed	**B** distinguished	**C** compared	**D** contrasted
11	**A** assembly	**B** formation	**C** build	**D** scheme
12	**A** protect	**B** retain	**C** restrict	**D** stock

For questions 13–27, read the text below and think of the word which best fits each gap. Use only one word in each gap. There is an example at the beginning (0).

Write your answers IN CAPITAL LETTERS on the separate answer sheet.

Example:

| 0 | P | L | A | C | E | | | | | | | | |

WORLD BOOK DAY

This year's World Book Day (WBD), which is taking 0 *place* on March 2, hopes to encourage everyone, and especially children, to discover the joy of reading.

Schools and libraries are getting involved, with a packed schedule of events designed 13 *to* bring books to life. 14 *There* will be writers popping 15 *into* schools to read from their books and answer questions, and story-telling events. Children will also be able to take 16 *part* in readings 17 *while/so* that they really have a chance to engage with the books.

18 *As* a further incentive to pick up a book, WBD has joined forces with National Book Tokens to offer schoolchildren a free £1 book token. The token can be put 19 *off/towards* the cost of any book or audio book 20 *of* their choice, or used to buy one of the six WBD £1 books. These books have been specially chosen 21 *because* of their appeal to different age groups.

As 22 *well* as hoping to encourage/get children to catch the reading bug, WBD also hopes to 23 *attract/get* reluctant adults hooked on books. So, 24 *for* the first time, World Book Day will also 25 *have* an adult focus, with the launch of Quick Reads, 26 *a* selection of short, fast-paced stories by well-known authors. The first set of Quick Reads will be published on World Book Day, 27 *after/with* a further collection of books being released later in the summer.

PART 3

For questions 28–37, read the text below. Use the word given in capitals at the end of some of the lines to form a word that fits in the gap in the same line. There is an example at the beginning (0).

Write your answers IN CAPITAL LETTERS *on the separate answer sheet.*

Example:

0	E	F	F	E	C	T	I	V	E			

NORDIC WALKING

Nordic walking is an 0 _____ technique that uses poles to bring
the upper body into more use and boost the calorie-burning effects of
walking. It was 28 _____ *originally* ✓ devised in Finland by elite cross-country
skiers as a way to keep their fitness levels up during the summer.
Although it has been in 29 _____ *existence* ✓ since the 1930s, it was only formally
developed as a sport in 1997. But far from being a 30 _____ *minoritory* ✓ sport, it
has grown rapidly in popularity and is now practised by around six million
people all over Europe.

    At first 31 _____ *sight* ✓ , Nordic walking may look like skiing without the
skis – or the snow. But although, to the 32 _____ *trained* ✗ eye, striding around
the local park with a pair of poles may look a bit silly, it actually offers a
serious 33 _____ *work-out* ✓ for people of all ages and abilities. You don't
34 _____ *necessarily* ✓ have to go faster to get more out of it – just put in more effort
with the poles. The poles, which can be made from aluminium or carbon
fibre, are specially designed to 35 _____ *maximise* ✗ the work done by the upper
body. And because Nordic walking is also a weight-bearing exercise, it's
great for 36 _____ *strenthing   streughening* bones and joints. But the best news is that because
the effort is spread across the 37 _____ *entreless   entirety* of the body, Nordic walking can
actually feel easier and less tiring than normal walking.

EFFECT

ORIGIN

EXIST

MINOR

SEE

TRAIN

WORK

NECESSARY

MAXIMUM

STRONG

ENTIRE

For questions 38–42, think of one word only which can be used appropriately in all three sentences. Here is an example (0).

Example:

0 If you're _____ next weekend, perhaps we could get together then.

This seat is _____ if you want to sit on it.

Feel _____ to stay with us any time you need a place to stay.

Example:

0	F	R	E	E								

Write only the missing word IN CAPITAL LETTERS *on the separate answer sheet.*

---

38 After long negotiations, they _____ *settled* the dispute without going to a court of law.

We looked at lots of apartments to rent and finally we ~~stayed~~ _____ on this one.

My family moved to Canada and ~~stayed~~ _____ in Toronto many years ago.

39 The last *part* _____ of the book isn't quite as exciting as the rest of it.

He always plays the _____ of the hero in his films.

Because one small _____ stopped working, the whole machine broke down.

40 I felt *fine* _____ when I got up this morning but I don't feel too good now.

There is a _____ line between perfectionism and obsession.

If you want to change our arrangement, that's _____ with me.

41 He got the job because he had a useful *contact* _____ in the company who arranged an interview for him.

We used to phone each other regularly, but I haven't been in _____ with her for some time.

In my job I have personal _____ with members of the public every day.

42 Could you _____ me at the next corner? I can walk from there.

The temperature tends to _____ sharply at night at this time of year.

I think we should _____ this subject before we have a big argument about it.

PART 5

For questions 43–50, complete the second sentence so that it has a similar meaning to the first sentence, using the word given. Do not change the word given. *You must use between* three *and* six *words, including the word given. Here is an example (0).*

Example:

0 I didn't know the way there, so I got lost.

GET

Not _____ there, I got lost.

0	K	N	O	W	I	N	G		H	O	W		T	O		G	E	T

Write the missing words IN CAPITAL LETTERS *on the separate answer sheet.*

---

43 Can anyone solve this problem?

COME

Can anyone _____ to this problem?

44 I'm sure you're wondering why I haven't contacted you for so long.

HAS

You must _____ so long since I contacted you.

45 Are you saying that I'm lying about what happened?

TRUTH

Are you accusing _____ about what happened?

46 He made a very quick decision and he didn't think about the matter enough.

WITHOUT

He made a very quick decision _____ to the matter.

47 Recently, the number of people who are out of work has gone down.

DECREASE

Recently, _____ the number of people who are out of work.

48 It doesn't matter how badly he behaved, you shouldn't have been so rude to him.

HOWEVER

You shouldn't have been so rude to him, _____ was.

49 I really regret making such a stupid mistake!

ONLY

If _____ such a stupid mistake!

50 Why are the two figures different?

ACCOUNTS

What _____ between the two figures?

Paper 4: Listening (40 minutes)

You will hear three different extracts. For questions 1–6, choose the answer (A, B or C) which fits best according to what you hear. There are two questions for each extract.

Extract one
You hear two people talking.

1   What is the situation?
   A   They have treated someone unfairly.
   B   They have fallen out with someone.
   C   They have changed their view of someone.

| 1 |

2   How do the speakers feel about the situation?
   A   resigned
   B   distressed
   C   puzzled

| 2 |

Extract two
You hear two people on the radio discussing a letter from a listener.

3   What is the first speaker doing when he speaks?
   A   suggesting that a problem is common
   B   expressing sympathy about someone's problem
   C   giving an objective account of a problem

| 3 |

4   The second speaker suggests that Paul should
   A   accept that some people are unkind to others.
   B   change his own attitude towards certain people.
   C   confront the people who have upset him.

| 4 |

Extract three
You hear two people talking about jokes and comedy.

5   The first speaker says that punchlines
   A   come in jokes that have formal structures.
   B   tend to be funnier than catchphrases.
   C   are easier to understand than in-jokes.

| 5 |

6   The second speaker says that many professional comedians
   A   try to cause events that they can make jokes about.
   B   exaggerate events that have actually happened to them.
   C   become confused about what is fact and what is fiction.

| 6 |

You will hear a reviewer talking about a new book on the subject of children's literature. For questions 7–14, complete the sentences.

AN ANTHOLOGY OF CHILDREN'S LITERATURE

The 1845 book *Slovenly Peter* had a character in it called [_____ 7].

The intended audience for the new anthology is [_____ 8].

The anthology includes books for teaching the [_____ 9] as well as story books.

Some of the stories in the anthology have [_____ 10].

The idea behind most early children's books was that children would learn [_____ 11] from them.

A children's book in 1744 had different [_____ 12] that came with it.

The anthology shows that lullabies from different cultures almost always deal with [_____ 13].

After the middle of the 18th century, it was no longer assumed that children were naturally [_____ 14] and children's literature changed.

UNIVERSITY *of* **CAMBRIDGE**
ESOL Examinations

Candidate Name
If not already printed, write name
in CAPITALS and complete the
Candidate No. grid (in pencil).

Candidate Signature

Examination Title

Centre

SAMPLE

Centre No.

Candidate No.

Examination Details

Supervisor:

If the candidate is ABSENT or has WITHDRAWN shade here

0	0	0	0
1	1	1	1
2	2	2	2
3	3	3	3
4	4	4	4
5	5	5	5
6	6	6	6
7	7	7	7
8	8	8	8
9	9	9	9

Candidate Answer Sheet

Instructions

Use a PENCIL (B or HB).

Mark ONE letter for each question.

For example, if you think B is the right answer to the question, mark your answer sheet like this:

0 A B C D E F G H

Rub out any answer you wish to change using an eraser.

1	A B C D E F G H
2	A B C D E F G H
3	A B C D E F G H
4	A B C D E F G H
5	A B C D E F G H
6	A B C D E F G H
7	A B C D E F G H
8	A B C D E F G H
9	A B C D E F G H
10	A B C D E F G H
11	A B C D E F G H
12	A B C D E F G H
13	A B C D E F G H
14	A B C D E F G H
15	A B C D E F G H
16	A B C D E F G H
17	A B C D E F G H
18	A B C D E F G H
19	A B C D E F G H
20	A B C D E F G H

21	A B C D E F G H
22	A B C D E F G H
23	A B C D E F G H
24	A B C D E F G H
25	A B C D E F G H
26	A B C D E F G H
27	A B C D E F G H
28	A B C D E F G H
29	A B C D E F G H
30	A B C D E F G H
31	A B C D E F G H
32	A B C D E F G H
33	A B C D E F G H
34	A B C D E F G H
35	A B C D E F G H
36	A B C D E F G H
37	A B C D E F G H
38	A B C D E F G H
39	A B C D E F G H
40	A B C D E F G H

A-H 40 CAS

denote
Print Limited 0121 520 5100

DP594/300

UNIVERSITY of CAMBRIDGE
ESOL Examinations

Do not write in this box

Candidate Name
If not already printed, write name
in CAPITALS and complete the
Candidate No. grid (in pencil).

Candidate Signature

SAMPLE

Examination Title

Centre

Centre No.

Candidate No.

Examination
Details

0	0	0	0
1	1	1	1
2	2	2	2
3	3	3	3
4	4	4	4
5	5	5	5
6	6	6	6
7	7	7	7
8	8	8	8
9	9	9	9

Supervisor:
If the candidate is ABSENT or has WITHDRAWN shade here

Instructions
Use a PENCIL (B or HB).
Rub out any answer you wish to change.

Part 1: Mark ONE letter for each question.

For example, if you think B is the right answer to
the question,
mark your answer
sheet like this:

Parts 2, 3, 4 and **5:** Write your answer
clearly in CAPITAL LETTERS.

For Parts 2, 3 and 4, write
one letter in each box.

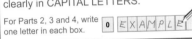

Candidate Answer Sheet

Part 2

Do not write
below here

13	13 1 0 u
14	14 1 0 u
15	15 1 0 u
16	16 1 0 u
17	17 1 0 u
18	18 1 0 u
19	19 1 0 u
20	20 1 0 u
21	21 1 0 u
22	22 1 0 u
23	23 1 0 u
24	24 1 0 u
25	25 1 0 u
26	26 1 0 u
27	27 1 0 u

Part 1

1	A	B	C	D
2	A	B	C	D
3	A	B	C	D
4	A	B	C	D
5	A	B	C	D
6	A	B	C	D
7	A	B	C	D
8	A	B	C	D
9	A	B	C	D
10	A	B	C	D
11	A	B	C	D
12	A	B	C	D

Continues over ➡

DP597/301

CAE UoE

Part 3

28	28 1 0 u
29	29 1 0 u
30	30 1 0 u
31	31 1 0 u
32	32 1 0 u
33	33 1 0 u
34	34 1 0 u
35	35 1 0 u
36	36 1 0 u
37	37 1 0 u

SAMPLE

Part 4

38	38 1 0 u
39	39 1 0 u
40	40 1 0 u
41	41 1 0 u
42	42 1 0 u

Part 5

43	43 2 1 0 u
44	44 2 1 0 u
45	45 2 1 0 u
46	46 2 1 0 u
47	47 2 1 0 u
48	48 2 1 0 u
49	49 2 1 0 u
50	50 2 1 0 u

denote Print Limited 0121 520 5100

UNIVERSITY *of* **CAMBRIDGE**
ESOL Examinations

Do not write in this box

Candidate Name
If not already printed, write name
in CAPITALS and complete the
Candidate No. grid (in pencil).

Candidate Signature

SAMPLE

Examination Title

Centre

Centre No.

Candidate No.

Examination
Details

0	0	0	0
1	1	1	1
2	2	2	2
3	3	3	3
4	4	4	4
5	5	5	5
6	6	6	6
7	7	7	7
8	8	8	8
9	9	9	9

Supervisor:

If the candidate is ABSENT or has WITHDRAWN shade here

Test version: A B C D E F J K L M N   Special arrangements: S H

Candidate Answer Sheet

Instructions

Use a PENCIL (B or HB).
Rub out any answer you wish to change using an eraser.

Parts 1, 3 and 4:
Mark ONE letter for each question.

For example, if you think **B** is the
right answer to the question, mark
your answer sheet like this:

0 A B C

Part 2:
Write your answer clearly in CAPITAL LETTERS.

Write one letter or number in each box.
If the answer has more than one word, leave one
box empty between words.

For example:

0 N U M B E R   1 2

Turn this sheet over to start.

DP600/304
CAE L

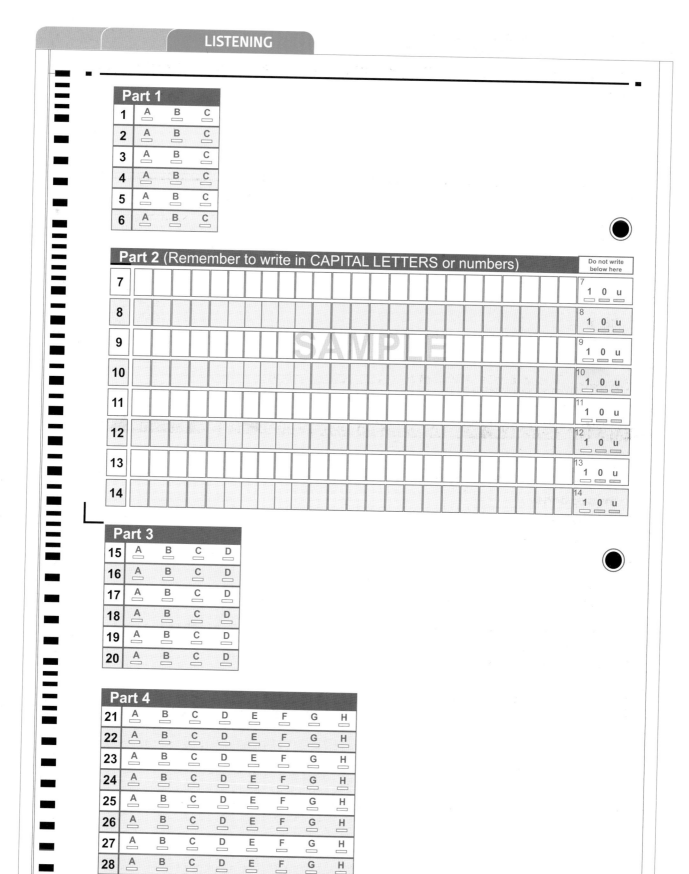

Part 1

1	A	B	C
2	A	B	C
3	A	B	C
4	A	B	C
5	A	B	C
6	A	B	C

Part 2 (Remember to write in CAPITAL LETTERS or numbers)

Do not write below here

7		7 1 0 u
8		8 1 0 u
9		9 1 0 u
10		10 1 0 u
11		11 1 0 u
12		12 1 0 u
13		13 1 0 u
14		14 1 0 u

Part 3

15	A	B	C	D
16	A	B	C	D
17	A	B	C	D
18	A	B	C	D
19	A	B	C	D
20	A	B	C	D

Part 4

21	A	B	C	D	E	F	G	H
22	A	B	C	D	E	F	G	H
23	A	B	C	D	E	F	G	H
24	A	B	C	D	E	F	G	H
25	A	B	C	D	E	F	G	H
26	A	B	C	D	E	F	G	H
27	A	B	C	D	E	F	G	H
28	A	B	C	D	E	F	G	H
29	A	B	C	D	E	F	G	H
30	A	B	C	D	E	F	G	H

TEST 1

Paper 1: Reading

PART 1 [ ] 12
PART 2 [ ] 12
PART 3 [ ] 14
PART 4 [ ] 15

Total [ ] 53   Score [ ] 40

Candidate score x 7.5 ÷ 10 = score out of 40
Example: 45 marks out of 53 = 34 marks out of 40 approximately

Paper 2: Writing

PART 1 [ ] 20
PART 2 [ ] 20

Total [ ] 40   Score [ ] 40

Paper 3: Use of English

PART 1 [ ] 12
PART 2 [ ] 15
PART 3 [ ] 10
PART 4 [ ] 10
PART 5 [ ] 16

Total [ ] 63   Score [ ] 40

Candidate score x 5 ÷ 8 = score out of 40
Example: 50 marks out of 63 = 31 marks out of 40 approximately

Paper 4: Listening

PART 1 [ ] 6
PART 2 [ ] 8
PART 3 [ ] 6
PART 4 [ ] 10

Total [ ] 30   Score [ ] 40

Candidate score ÷ 3 x 4 = score out of 40
Example: 24 marks out of 30 = 32 marks out of 40

Paper 5: Speaking

Total [ ] 20   Score [ ] 40

Candidate score x 2 = score out of 40

Test total [ ] 200
÷ 2 = [ ] %
Approximate grade (see below) [ ]

TEST 2

Paper 1: Reading

PART 1 [ ] 12
PART 2 [ ] 12
PART 3 [ ] 14
PART 4 [ ] 15

Total [ ] 53   Score [ ] 40

Candidate score x 7.5 ÷ 10 = score out of 40
Example: 45 marks out of 53 = 34 marks out of 40 approximately

Paper 2: Writing

PART 1 [ ] 20
PART 2 [ ] 20

Total [ ] 40   Score [ ] 40

Paper 3: Use of English

PART 1 [ ] 12
PART 2 [ ] 15
PART 3 [ ] 10
PART 4 [ ] 10
PART 5 [ ] 16

Total [ ] 63   Score [ ] 40

Candidate score x 5 ÷ 8 = score out of 40
Example: 50 marks out of 63 = 31 marks out of 40 approximately

Paper 4: Listening

PART 1 [ ] 6
PART 2 [ ] 8
PART 3 [ ] 6
PART 4 [ ] 10

Total [ ] 30   Score [ ] 40

Candidate score ÷ 3 x 4 = score out of 40
Example: 24 marks out of 30 = 32 marks out of 40

Paper 5: Speaking

Total [ ] 20   Score [ ] 40

Candidate score x 2 = score out of 40

Test total [ ] 200
÷ 2 = [ ] %
Approximate grade (see below) [ ]

Approximate percentages for grades A–E

Pass   A 80% and above   **Fail**   D 55–59%
           B 75–79%   E 54% and below
           C 60–74%

TEST 3

Paper 1: Reading

PART 1 ☐ 12
PART 2 ☐ 12
PART 3 ☐ 14
PART 4 ☐ 15

Total ☐ 53   Score ☐ 40

Candidate score x 7.5 ÷ 10 = score out of 40
Example: 45 marks out of 53 = 34 marks out of 40 approximately

Paper 2: Writing

PART 1 ☐ 20
PART 2 ☐ 20

Total ☐ 40   Score ☐ 40

Paper 3: Use of English

PART 1 ☐ 12
PART 2 ☐ 15
PART 3 ☐ 10
PART 4 ☐ 10
PART 5 ☐ 16

Total ☐ 63   Score ☐ 40

Candidate score x 5 ÷ 8 = score out of 40
Example: 50 marks out of 63 = 31 marks out of 40 approximately

Paper 4: Listening

PART 1 ☐ 6
PART 2 ☐ 8
PART 3 ☐ 6
PART 4 ☐ 10

Total ☐ 30   Score ☐ 40

Candidate score ÷ 3 x 4 = score out of 40
Example: 24 marks out of 30 = 32 marks out of 40

Paper 5: Speaking

Total ☐ 20   Score ☐ 40

Candidate score x 2 = score out of 40

Test total ☐ 200
÷ 2 = ☐ %
Approximate grade (see below) ☐

Approximate percentages for grades A–E
Pass   A 80% and above   **Fail**   D 55–59%
           B 75–79%   E 54% and below
           C 60–74%

TEST 4

Paper 1: Reading

PART 1 ☐ 12
PART 2 ☐ 12
PART 3 ☐ 14
PART 4 ☐ 15

Total ☐ 53   Score ☐ 40

Candidate score x 7.5 ÷ 10 = score out of 40
Example: 45 marks out of 53 = 34 marks out of 40 approximately

Paper 2: Writing

PART 1 ☐ 20
PART 2 ☐ 20

Total ☐ 40   Score ☐ 40

Paper 3: Use of English

PART 1 ☐ 12
PART 2 ☐ 15
PART 3 ☐ 10
PART 4 ☐ 10
PART 5 ☐ 16

Total ☐ 63   Score ☐ 40

Candidate score x 5 ÷ 8 = score out of 40
Example: 50 marks out of 63 = 31 marks out of 40 approximately

Paper 4: Listening

PART 1 ☐ 6
PART 2 ☐ 8
PART 3 ☐ 6
PART 4 ☐ 10

Total ☐ 30   Score ☐ 40

Candidate score ÷ 3 x 4 = score out of 40
Example: 24 marks out of 30 = 32 marks out of 40

Paper 5: Speaking

Total ☐ 20   Score ☐ 40

Candidate score x 2 = score out of 40

Test total ☐ 200
÷ 2 = ☐ %
Approximate grade (see below) ☐

Assessing the Writing paper

Students' answers are assessed with reference to two mark schemes: one based on the overall impression; the other on the requirements of the particular task.

The General impression mark scheme refers to the content, organization and cohesion, range of structures and vocabulary, accuracy, register and format, and the target reader indicated in the task.

The Task specific mark scheme in the Answer key lists the above criteria specific to each particular task and explains what is required in each answer. Teachers should assess the answer under the Task specific mark scheme and then award an overall General impression band mark and a score out of 20.

Candidates who fully satisfy the Band 3 descriptor will demonstrate an adequate performance in writing at CAE level.

General impression mark scheme

BAND 5 *(approximately 17–20 marks)*

For a Band 5 to be awarded, the candidate's writing has a very positive effect on the target reader. The content is relevant and the topic is fully developed. Information and ideas are skilfully organized through a range of cohesive devices, which are used to good effect. A wide range of complex structures and vocabulary is used effectively. Errors are minimal, and inaccuracies which do occur have no impact on communication. Register and format are consistently appropriate to the purpose of the task and the audience.

BAND 4 *(approximately 13–16 marks)*

For a Band 4 to be awarded, the candidate's writing has a positive effect on the target reader. The content is relevant and the topic is developed. Information and ideas are clearly organized through the use of a variety of cohesive devices. A good range of complex structures and vocabulary is used. Some errors may occur with vocabulary and when complex language is attempted, but these do not cause difficulty for the reader. Register and format are usually appropriate to the purpose of the task and the audience.

BAND 3 *(approximately 8–12 marks)*

For a Band 3 to be awarded, the candidate's writing has a satisfactory effect on the target reader. The content is relevant with some development of the topic. Information and ideas are generally organized logically, though cohesive devices may not always be used appropriately. A satisfactory range of structures and vocabulary is used, though word choice may lack precision. Errors which do occur do not cause difficulty for the reader. Register and format are reasonably appropriate to the purpose of the task and the audience.

BAND 2 *(approximately 4–7 marks)*

For a Band 2 to be awarded, the candidate's writing has a negative effect on the target reader. The content is not always relevant. Information and ideas are inadequately organized and sometimes incoherent, with inaccurate use of cohesive devices. The range of structures and vocabulary is limited and/ or repetitive, and errors may be basic or cause difficulty for the reader. Register and format are sometimes inappropriate to the purpose of the task and the audience.

BAND 1 *(approximately 1–3 marks)*

For a Band 1 to be awarded, the candidate's writing has a very negative effect on the target reader. The content is often irrelevant. Information and ideas are poorly organized, often incoherent, and there is minimal use of cohesive devices. The range of structures and vocabulary is severely limited, and errors frequently cause considerable difficulty for the reader. Register and format are inappropriate to the purpose of the task and the audience.

BAND 0 *(no marks)*

For a Band zero to be awarded, there is either too little language for assessment or the candidate's writing is totally irrelevant or illegible. Candidates who do not address all the content points will be penalized for dealing inadequately with the requirements of the task.

Assessing the Speaking paper

Assessment (out of 20 marks) is based on performance in the whole test, and is not related to performance in particular parts of the test. Students are assessed on their own individual performance and not in relation to each other.

Marks are awarded by the assessor, who does not take part in the test, according to five analytical criteria: *Grammatical Resource*, *Vocabulary Resource*, *Discourse Management*, *Pronunciation*, and *Interactive Communication*. The interlocutor, who conducts the test, gives a mark for *Global Achievement*.

GRAMMATICAL RESOURCE

This refers to the accurate and appropriate use of a range of both simple and complex forms. Performance is viewed in terms of the overall effectiveness of the language used in spoken interaction.

VOCABULARY RESOURCE

This refers to the candidate's ability to use a range of vocabulary to meet task requirements. At CAE level, the tasks require candidates to speculate and exchange views on unfamiliar topics. Performance is viewed in terms of the overall effectiveness of the language used in spoken interaction.

DISCOURSE MANAGEMENT

This refers to the candidate's ability to link utterances together to form coherent speech, without undue hesitation. The utterances should be relevant to the tasks and should be arranged logically to develop the themes or arguments required by the tasks.

PRONUNCIATION

This refers to the candidate's ability to produce intelligible utterances to fulfil the task requirements. This includes stress and intonation as well as individual sounds. Examiners put themselves in the position of a non-ESOL specialist and assess the overall impact of the pronunciation and the degree of effort required to understand the candidate.

INTERACTIVE COMMUNICATION

This refers to the candidate's ability to take an active part in the development of the discourse. This requires an ability to participate in the range of interactive situations in the test and to develop discussions on a range of topics by initiating and responding appropriately. This also refers to the deployment of strategies to maintain interaction at an appropriate level throughout the test so that the tasks can be fulfilled.

GLOBAL ACHIEVEMENT

This refers to the candidate's overall effectiveness in dealing with the tasks in the four separate parts of the CAE Speaking test. The global mark is an independent impression mark which reflects the assessment of the candidate's performance from the interlocutor's perspective.

For an explanation of how marks are calculated, see page 100.

TEST 1

Paper 1: Reading

PART 1

1 A	4 C
2 C	5 D
3 B	6 B

PART 2

7 G	10 A
8 B	11 F
9 E	12 D

PART 3

13 C	17 A
14 A	18 B
15 B	19 B
16 D	

PART 4

20 E	28 D
21 B	29 E
22 B	30 A
23 / 24 A / B	31 / 32 A / C
25 C	33 E
26 / 27 A / D	34 D

Paper 2: Writing

For General impression mark scheme, see page 102.

QUESTION 1 *Task specific mark scheme*

Content

The article should contain brief general descriptions of the main newspapers, perhaps in different categories if this is possible. It should summarize the main features of the papers, and include the writer's opinions on one or more of them. It is not necessary to include all of the bullet points in the list of notes (they are described as 'possible' things to include).

Range of grammar and vocabulary

It is likely that the accurate use of comparative structures is required, in addition to the appropriate use of passive structures and the appropriate, mostly present simple, verb tenses. Vocabulary appropriate to describing types of newspaper and the content of newspapers is required, as well as vocabulary for giving opinions on them.

Register

The register should be mostly neutral, because the article contains description / analysis of something factual. Where opinions are given, the register may be more informal.

Organization and cohesion

The article should be divided appropriately into paragraphs, dealing with different types of newspaper or aspects of the newspapers discussed. Separate paragraphs may be used for the bullet points in the list of notes that the writer chooses to include. Opinions may come in a separate paragraph or within each paragraph. Appropriate linking words and phrases should be used for comparing (e.g. *whereas*), for contrasting (e.g. *however*, *although*), for exemplifying (e.g. *for example*) and for giving reasons (e.g. *because*).

Target reader

The reader should have a clear picture of what the national newspapers in the writer's country are like, and should learn other information about them such as which ones are most popular or what kind of people read different ones. The reader should also be clear as to the writer's opinions on the papers.

Model answer

THE NATIONAL NEWSPAPERS IN MY COUNTRY

The national newspapers in my country can be divided into two main categories – broadsheets and tabloids. The broadsheet newspapers are big and the tabloids are the same size as magazines.

In general terms, the broadsheets are serious newspapers, which mainly contain news from the country and abroad, and comment on that news. The tabloids focus less on actual news and more on either gossip about celebrities or controversial social issues. The broadsheets are written in a sophisticated style, whereas the tabloids are more sensational and written in the sort of language that ordinary people might use.

The broadsheets are generally read by people who are interested in the news and in politics and who want to spend some time reading their newspaper, whereas the tabloids are read by people who want a bit of entertainment, for example on their way to work or during a break at work. You have to concentrate to read a broadsheet, whereas it's easy to read a tabloid quickly.

Although I don't have any statistics to support this, I believe that more people buy tabloids than the other categories of paper. I usually read one of the tabloids because it's entertaining and I find the other kinds of paper rather dull.

QUESTION 2 *Task specific mark scheme*

Content

The review should describe the product in some detail and give the writer's opinions on it, including whether or not the writer recommends it.

Range of grammar and vocabulary

The review should include appropriate structures for describing the writer's experience with the product, including appropriate past and present tenses. Appropriate structures for giving opinions and recommending should also be used. Vocabulary associated with buying and using products should be used accurately, as well as vocabulary connected with the particular product chosen.

Register

The review may be neutral or fairly informal. The writer may be completely objective about the product, or take a more personal, informal approach.

Organization and cohesion

The review may be divided into paragraphs separating a description of the product from the writer's opinions of it. The background, for example explaining why the writer bought the product, where the writer came across it, etc. may be included, perhaps as a separate paragraph. The product itself must be identified at the beginning, perhaps in a title for the review. Linking words and phrases should be used appropriately, perhaps to link stages in a sequence of events or to link opinions with reasons for them.

Target reader

The reader should have a clear idea of exactly what the product is and what the writer thinks of it.

Model answer

THE GEORGETOWN SHELVING SYSTEM

I recently purchased this product, having seen it widely advertised. As my apartment is quite small and I have quite a large number of books, DVDs and CDs, I was looking for something that would save space and enable me to keep everything in a neat and tidy way in one place. The pictures of the shelving system in the adverts made it look ideal for someone in this situation, as did the price, which is significantly below that of other, comparable, products.

I bought the product online and had it delivered to me. The shelving system came in three separate boxes and it required self-assembly. When I had removed everything from the boxes, I was initially concerned as to whether I would be able to put it together myself. The plans looked complicated and time-consuming, and this kind of thing is not one of my strengths. However, I embarked on the process, and was both surprised and pleased to discover forty-five minutes later that I had completed the process and my shelving system was ready for use.

I then organized and put away all the items that have been lying around in a mess in my apartment for some time. I was able to place the shelving system along one wall and put everything neatly into it. The system enables you

to store an enormous number of items in a relatively small space and it has transformed my apartment. I heartily recommend it to anyone who needs to save space – it is cleverly designed and extremely good value for money.

QUESTION 3 *Task specific mark scheme*

Content

The proposal must contain details of what the event would be, where it would take place, what it would involve and how it could be organized. It should also make clear what the scenario is, for example the kind of establishment that is celebrating its anniversary.

Range of grammar and vocabulary

It is likely that the proposal will need to include accurate use of modals such as *would*, *could*, etc. to talk about possibilities and arrangements for the event. Appropriate structures for recommending and suggesting should be used accurately. Vocabulary connected with the kind of event suggested should be used accurately.

Register

The proposal should be fairly formal or neutral because the context is fairly formal – the writer is submitting a proposal to people who are in charge.

Organization and cohesion

The proposal should be appropriately organized in paragraphs or sections, which may each be given a title. These should deal with different aspects, for example the background, the nature of the proposed event and reasons for choosing it, and suggestions for how it can be organized. Appropriate linking of points should be present.

Target reader

The reader would understand clearly the kind of event being proposed, what that event would involve and how it could be organized.

Model answer

20TH ANNIVERSARY EVENT

A Reunion

My suggestion is that the event should be primarily a social one that involves both the past and the present. Since the school opened, former students have gone on to do all sorts of interesting things, and the school has maintained contact with many of them. I think we should stage a reunion of as many of these people as possible, to bring them back together with members of staff they knew from their time here and introduce them to current members of staff who joined after their time here.

The Event

The event that I am proposing would be a party / dinner in the Main Hall. We would employ outside caterers to provide the food and we can decide in due course whether this should be a buffet or a sit-down meal. We can also decide later on the precise number of people to invite, but I suggest that a maximum of about 100 would be appropriate. I suggest that the event should include one or two speeches. One speech should be given by the Principal, and I suggest that we ask one of the former students also to give a speech, in which they recall their time here.

An Exhibition

I propose that a further ingredient of the event should be an exhibition of photographs and other items connected with the history of the school since it opened. The exhibition should be arranged chronologically to provide an interesting, and perhaps amusing, look back over the years. I believe that we can select suitable photos and items from the records kept by the school.

QUESTION 4 *Task specific mark scheme*

Content

The essay must fully address the points made in both statements – both that work and education should be fun and that people cannot do them well if they are not fun.

Range of grammar and vocabulary

Appropriate active and passive verb tenses should be used accurately, as should appropriate adverb forms for describing how people do things. It is likely that the accurate use of both conditional structures and comparative structures is also required. Vocabulary connected with work or education should be used accurately, and vocabulary describing feelings and attitudes should also be used accurately.

Register

The essay may be neutral, fairly formal or fairly informal, depending on the approach the writer chooses to take to the topic.

Organization and cohesion

The essay should have an appropriate introduction and an appropriate conclusion. It should be appropriately divided into paragraphs. This may involve a paragraph or paragraphs agreeing with the statements and a paragraph or paragraphs disagreeing, or agreement and disagreement may be combined within paragraphs. Appropriate linking words and phrases should be used for linking related points and for linking points with supporting reasons for them.

Target reader

The reader should understand fully the writer's views on the topic, and the arguments that the writer puts forward in support of those views.

Model answer

It is of course true that people are happier if they enjoy their work or education, but in my view it is not necessarily true that they cannot learn or work effectively unless they are having fun.

These days, the idea that work and education have to be 'fun' is widespread in some countries. In other places, people assume that education and work may be hard and not at all fun. These people regard education and work as things that simply have to be done, and they do not expect them to be particularly enjoyable. Some people believe that the more you enjoy doing something, the better you do it, but I do not believe that this is always the case. Plenty of people do jobs they don't enjoy but they do them very effectively because that is what is expected of them and that is what they expect of themselves. They do their jobs well because that is what they are being paid to do, and enjoyment is not the main thing on their minds. Equally, many people do well in their education because they want to be successful and therefore they study hard, not because they particularly enjoy studying.

In my opinion, the word 'essential' should be changed to 'desirable' in the first sentence. Of course, it would be great if everyone could do things that they really enjoy, but the reality is that not everyone can. I think it's a bonus if you can spend your time doing things that are fun, not a requirement.

Paper 3: Use of English

PART 1

1	B	5	D	9	D
2	C	6	D	10	A
3	A	7	B	11	B
4	A	8	C	12	C

PART 2

13 your
14 about
15 most / greatest / biggest
16 over
17 of
18 not
19 take / have
20 it
21 longer
22 comes
23 way
24 even
25 better
26 Although / Though/ While / Whilst
27 at

28 annoyance
29 bearing
30 reference
31 emotional
32 honesty

33 workings
34 Existing
35 offence
36 disclose
37 truthful

PART 4

38 chance
39 excuse
40 late

41 place
42 meet

PART 5

43 there's / there is][**hardly** any petrol
44 had no **idea** (that)][cars cost
45 **let** it][get you
46 to be][making a **recovery**
47 take her work seriously enough,][according
48 of his **inability**][to do
49 can't / cannot be **bothered**][to have
50 causing you][such a **lot** of

Paper 4: Listening

PART 1

1 B
2 C
3 A

4 B
5 A
6 A

PART 2

7 melted
8 mass(-)producing
9 (some) popcorn
10 exploded

11 a restaurant
12 a competition
13 meat
14 counter

PART 3

15 B
16 A
17 D

18 B
19 C
20 C

PART 4

21 G
22 C
23 E
24 A

25 H
26 C
27 F
28 H

29 D
30 A

Paper 5: Speaking

Teachers should use their own judgement to award marks out of 20 based on the assessment criteria on page 103.

TEST 2

Paper 1: Reading

PART 1

1 C
2 B
3 D

4 A
5 C
6 B

PART 2

7 E
8 G
9 C

10 A
11 F
12 B

PART 3

13 B
14 C
15 D
16 B

17 A
18 B
19 A

PART 4

20 B
21 C
22 A
23 B
24 D

25 A
26 A
27 B
28 D
29 D

30 B
31 C
32 C
33 B
34 D

Paper 2: Writing

For General impression mark scheme, see page 102.

<u>QUESTION 1</u> *Task specific mark scheme*

Content

The letter must describe the writer's experience of the adventure sports centre, and give the reader information and advice concerning his/her possible visit to it. Everything that the friend mentions in the letter should be addressed but it is not necessary or possible to include every single detail from the diary – the writer should choose which ones to include.

Range of grammar and vocabulary

Appropriate past tenses must be used accurately for describing the writer's experiences. Appropriate structures for giving advice and recommending must also be used. Vocabulary appropriate to the activities described should be used accurately, and vocabulary for describing feelings should also be used accurately.

Register

The register should be fairly informal because it is from one friend to another.

Organization and cohesion

The letter should be organized into appropriate paragraphs. There should be clear opening and closing paragraphs giving a brief summary relating to the writer's experience and the writer's advice to the friend. The description of the writer's own experience may be divided into suitable paragraphs. Suitable linking words and phrases should be used.

Target reader

The reader should be completely clear as to what the writer felt about his/her visit to the centre, what happened when he/she was there and whether the writer believes that the reader would enjoy visiting it.

Model answer

Dear Nick,
I think you'd really enjoy the place. I had a really good time there and I reckon you would too.

The scariest thing I did was diving. I got pretty worked up while I was doing that and couldn't carry on with it. We each had a qualified teacher with us, so I knew I was safe, but I panicked anyway and gave up. The canoeing was pretty scary too, but again there was a teacher looking after me the whole time so I didn't feel I was really in a lot of danger.

Apart from that, all the activities were great fun, even if some of them were pretty hard. The assault course, which I did on the first day, was extremely demanding but I enjoyed it and I think you would too. I was pretty useless at rock climbing at first, but I got the hang of it after a while and really enjoyed that. You really must try that!

There was a great bunch of people at the centre and we had a lot of fun together. Setting up a camp was hilarious – we got into a terrible mess. I'm sure I'll see some of them again.

I felt that I achieved a lot at the centre and that it was well worth going. I certainly think you should go too.

QUESTION 2 Task specific mark scheme

Content

The guidebook contribution must describe the building, say why it is notable, describe people's opinions of it and give information about visiting it.

Range of grammar and vocabulary

Appropriate present and past tenses should be used for describing the building and its history. Passive structures are likely to be required. Appropriate structures for describing other people's opinions of something should also be used accurately (e.g. be regarded as). Vocabulary associated with the appearance of buildings and places must be used accurately.

Register

The register should be neutral or fairly formal, as the context (writing a piece for a book) requires.

Organization and cohesion

The guidebook contribution should be organized appropriately into paragraphs. Different paragraphs may describe the history of the building, its physical appearance, opinions of it and details concerning visiting it. Appropriate linking words and phrases should be used within and between sentences and paragraphs.

Target reader

The reader should have a clear mental picture of what the building looks like, why it is worthy of inclusion in the book, what people think of it and the situation regarding visiting it.

Model answer

THE WHITEHEAD TOWER

The Whitehead Tower is now perhaps the most famous landmark in the city, and when it was constructed three years ago, it was certainly the most controversial new building in the city for many years.

The Tower is not only the tallest building in the city, it is the tallest building in the country. Its unusual shape has given rise to its local nickname 'The Guitar'. The top of the building is visible from just about any part of the city centre and it could be said to dominate the city. Critics describe it as an eyesore that does not fit in with the architecture of the city centre at all. Certainly, its steel and glass exterior contrast markedly with the older styles of architecture that characterize the majority of major buildings in the city.

The building certainly has many supporters, though. They say that a modern city needs the latest in modern architecture, and that the Whitehead Tower represents the right image of the city to others. They say that it reflects the fact that the city is a modern city for the modern age, a vibrant city with much to offer to young and ambitious people.

The Tower is mostly given over to offices, but certain parts of it are open to the public. Anyone can use the state-of-the-art gym on the ground floor, as well as the famous Tower Restaurant on the 50th floor, with its panoramic views over the city. Bookings are usually required for the restaurant because of its enormous popularity.

QUESTION 3 Task specific mark scheme

Content

The competition entry must describe three possessions, saying why they are so important to the writer and describing how or why they came into the writer's possession.

Range of grammar and vocabulary

Appropriate past and present verb tenses must be used throughout, and the present perfect tense is likely to be required to link the history of items with the present situation concerning them. Relative clauses are likely to be required to give information on the items. Vocabulary connected with each item must be used accurately, and vocabulary connected with feelings and memories should also be used accurately.

Register

The register could be informal, neutral or informal, depending on the approach the writer wishes to take. The announcement suggests that all three would be acceptable.

Organization and cohesion

The competition entry should be organized into appropriate paragraphs, probably one for each possession. Appropriate linking words and phrases should be used to link information about the possessions with reasons why they are important to the writer.

Target reader

The reader should understand fully what exactly the possessions are and why they are so precious to the writer.

Model answer

MY THREE MOST PRECIOUS POSSESSIONS

One of the possessions that is most precious to me is the photograph album I put together of photos of the trip around Europe that I took two years ago. The trip is the most enjoyable thing that I have ever done and the photographs bring back all sorts of memories of that wonderful time. When I look at them, I feel as if I am back in the fantastic places I went to. The photos remind me of some of the great adventures I had and some of the fascinating people I met.

Another of my most precious possessions is a ring that belonged to my great-grandfather, given to me many years ago by my grandmother. It isn't a particularly valuable ring and I never met my great-grandfather, but it's something I really treasure. From what people in the family have told me, he was an incredible man who had a fascinating life and it's great to have this link with the past.

The other possession that is most precious to me is the autograph of my favourite singer. He came to my city last year and I found out which hotel he was staying in. I stood outside the hotel for hours and eventually he came out to get into his car. I managed to speak to him and he was very friendly and agreed to sign his name on a piece of paper for me. He even wrote a special message for me. I was so thrilled.

Content

The report must address all the points listed – who the writer visited and when, what happened during the visit, how the visit compared with the earlier visit, and general comments on the exchange programme.

Range of grammar and vocabulary

Appropriate past tenses must be used accurately to describe the writer's visit and the earlier visit. Comparative structures are required to compare the two visits. Structures for giving opinions or recommending are required for the general comments. Vocabulary appropriate to the topic of visiting people and places must be used accurately, as should vocabulary for describing behaviour and feelings.

Register

The register should be fairly formal or neutral, as is appropriate for a report.

Organization and cohesion

The report should begin with an opening paragraph, briefly explaining the background. It should then be divided appropriately into paragraphs dealing with different aspects, for example the previous visit, the recent visit and general points about the programme. Each paragraph could be presented as a separate section with its own heading. Appropriate linking should be used for connecting causes with results (e.g. why the writer felt as he/she did), for comparing and contrasting (e.g. *whereas, although, however,* etc.), and perhaps for making further points (e.g. *in addition, as well as*).

Target reader

The reader should understand fully what both visits were like and what the writer's opinion of them is, as well as what the writer thinks of the programme in general and why.

Model answer

EXCHANGE VISIT TO LONDON

In July, I went to London to stay with Helen Oliver and her family for three weeks as part of the exchange programme. Helen had previously been to stay with me for three weeks in March.

Helen and her family made me feel welcome from the very beginning. I was told that I should make myself at home and come and go as I pleased. They provided wonderful meals and made me feel that I was part of the family. In view of all this, it may be unfair to criticize. However, the problem for me was that I had no idea what to do or where to go most of the time. Helen took me into the town once or twice but apart from that she didn't take me to any places of interest. I had to find things to do for myself, with little or no guidance, and as a result I felt that I wasted a lot of my time.

When Helen stayed with me, my family and I took her somewhere almost every day, and she commented on how much she had appreciated our efforts and how much she had learnt about our city. I had been expecting something similar to happen when I stayed with her.

So, although I enjoyed my trip in many ways, I recommend that it should be made clear to everyone taking part in the programme that they are expected to provide some sort of programme of activities for visitors, or at least give them the information they need to make the most of their stay.

Paper 3: Use of English

PART 1

1	C	5	D	9	C
2	A	6	A	10	A
3	D	7	A	11	D
4	C	8	B	12	B

PART 2

13	to	18	anything	23	from
14	how	19	an	24	great / good
15	being	20	then	25	so
16	and	21	do	26	that
17	its	22	by	27	for

PART 3

28	nomination	33	entry
29	receipt	34	evenly
30	diners	35	deadline
31	chosen	36	unannounced
32	contested	37	prestigious

PART 4

38	wrong	41	true
39	view	42	issue
40	treat		

PART 5

43 a **while**][before / until / till I fully
44 isn't / is not **worth**][arguing about
45 there be][any / a **delay**
46 made no **effort**][to give / offer me
47 have anything][in **common** with
48 have a private][**word** with
49 my amazement,][nothing **went**
50 wouldn't / would not **dream** of doing][any

Paper 4: Listening

PART 1

1	B	4	C
2	C	5	A
3	B	6	C

PART 2

7	radiator	11	cross
8	two-thirds / ⅔	12	buildings
9	travel	13	backgrounds
10	young adulthood	14	campus

PART 3

15	A	18	B
16	C	19	C
17	D	20	A

PART 4

21	G	25	A	29	A
22	D	26	E	30	H
23	B	27	G		
24	F	28	C		

Paper 5: Speaking

Teachers should use their own judgement to award marks out of 20 based on the assessment criteria on page 103.

TEST 3

Paper 1: Reading

PART 1

1	C	4	C
2	D	5	C
3	A	6	A

PART 2

7	E	10	F
8	G	11	D
9	B	12	C

PART 3

13	C	17	B
14	C	18	B
15	A	19	A
16	D		

PART 4

20	B	25	B	30	B
21	D	26	B	31	C
22	C	27	D	32	B
23	A	28	D	33	A
24	C	29	A	34	D

Paper 2: Writing

For General impression mark scheme, see page 102.

For General impression mark scheme, see page 102.

QUESTION 1 *Task specific mark scheme*

Content

The report must describe and comment on all the events. It cannot include every detail provided on the events and in the notes. Instead, it must select the appropriate event details and comments to create a coherent report that presents an analysis of the events and the writer's comments and conclusions on them.

Range of grammar and vocabulary

Appropriate past tenses to describe the events must be used accurately. Appropriate future tenses are required for future recommendations and conditional structures may be required both to talk about how the events could have been organized in the past and how they could be organized in the future. Vocabulary associated with organizing, staging events and profit and loss must be used accurately.

Register

The register should be neutral or fairly formal, as this is a report for a committee.

Organization and cohesion

The report should have an appropriate format, probably divided into sections dealing with each event. Descriptions of what happened should be linked with causes and results of what happened and recommendations relating to it by the appropriate use of linking words and phrases.

Target reader

The reader should be clear as to the main points concerning what happened for each event and what the writer has concluded concerning each event.

Model answer

REPORT ON ENTERTAINMENTS

Theatre Trip (19 March)

The choice of play was excellent – it was as funny as it had been described in the local paper. However, not many people came to the event, and because of the cost of hiring a coach to take us there, we lost money on the event. If we are to offer a similar trip in future, we will need to advertise more extensively so that we get enough people to make it viable financially.

Music Evening (20 June)

This event was very successful and very well attended. We were able to choose excellent bands to perform because there are so many talented bands locally. As a result, demand for tickets was high and we sold out of them before the event. The atmosphere at the event was excellent and it was enjoyed by everyone there. We made a big profit on this event.

Annual Party (1 August)

We need to change the way we organize this in future. We didn't sell tickets in advance and underestimated the number of people who would come. As a result, there were too many people and the Main Hall was overcrowded. On the other hand, the very varied food that was provided proved very popular and we were able to make a small profit on the event.

QUESTION 2 *Task specific mark scheme*

Content

The article should describe one or more future inventions, and give reasons why it would be good if it was or they were invented. It should mention the advantages of the invention(s) for the writer and / or people in general.

Range of grammar and vocabulary

The article is likely to require accurate use of modals (e.g. *would*, *could*, etc.) to describe future possibilities and wishes. Appropriate conditional structures may also be required, as may relative clauses to give further information on the inventions. Vocabulary connected with the kind of invention being described must be used accurately, and vocabulary connected with the advantages of something may also be required.

Register

The register can be fairly formal, neutral or fairly informal, depending on the approach the writer chooses to take. The topic and context mean that the article may be intended to make readers think or it may be intended to entertain or amuse readers.

Organization and cohesion

The article should be organized appropriately in paragraphs. These may each deal with different inventions or with different aspects of a single invention. Appropriate linking words and phrases should be used to link descriptions of the invention(s) with reasons why the invention(s) would be a good thing.

Target reader

The reader would understand fully what the invention(s) is / are and why the writer considers it desirable for it / them to be invented.

Model answer

THINGS THAT REALLY WORK

Although we live in a technological age, and there are devices to perform all sorts of functions, it seems to me that many of these things often don't work, and that this causes all sorts of annoyance and inconvenience. So I would like to see the invention of things that work properly all the time.

First of all, I would like to see the invention of the computer that never crashes. It seems to me that everyone assumes that from time to time their computer will not work properly or will not work at all. This causes a great deal of trouble, and the fact that computers are unreliable can of course affect not just individuals but many thousands of people. How many times do we hear that something that affects the public can be blamed on computer problems? This is a very serious problem that people don't seem to pay attention to. So I would like to see the invention of the computer that never goes wrong.

Similarly, I would like to see the invention of the car that never breaks down and the domestic appliance that always works. We all accept that we could be driving somewhere and at any point our cars might simply stop working, without warning, leaving us in a very difficult situation. In the same way, everyone is familiar with the experience of switching on something at home like a vacuum cleaner and finding that nothing happens. It has simply died, although it was working perfectly well the last time you used it. This kind of thing drives you mad.

QUESTION 3 *Task specific mark scheme*

Content
The review must explain who gave the performance and what the writer and audience thought of it. It must also compare the performance with the same person's / people's performances in recordings or on TV / in films.

Range of grammar and vocabulary
It is likely that a wide variety of verb tenses will be required – past tenses for the performance, and present and present perfect tenses for the background and the situation until the performance. Comparative structures are required to compare the live performance with the previously seen or heard performances. Vocabulary associated with performing and entertainment must be used accurately, and vocabulary describing people's feelings, impressions and reactions should also be used accurately.

Register
The register may be neutral, fairly informal or fairly formal. The writer may choose to write a serious review or to write a review that is intended simply to entertain the reader.

Organization and cohesion
The review should be appropriately divided into paragraphs, perhaps presenting the background, a description of the performance, a comparison with other performances and a conclusion. Appropriate linking words and phrases should be used to link description with opinion.

Target reader
The reader should have a clear idea of what the performance was like, what the writer and other people there thought of it and how it compared with previous performances in the writer's opinion.

Model answer
CONCERT REVIEW: THE HIGHLIGHTS
Recently I went to see The Highlights giving a concert at a huge stadium near my home town. The Highlights are one of the most popular bands here at the moment and they are also my favourite band. I've got everything they've ever recorded and I must have listened to each song at least a hundred times! However, until that concert I had never managed to see them live before. So I was incredibly excited about seeing them.

Their performance was certainly not a disappointment. They played all of their best-known songs but they didn't play them exactly as they sound on the CDs. The sound was not as sophisticated as it is on the recordings and there were none of the special effects from the records. Instead, what we saw and heard was the band playing and singing in a natural way, without much technology, as if they were performing in a local club. In my opinion, they sounded even better than they do on the recordings. There was more energy and it seemed somehow more personal. They didn't seem like a hugely famous act, remote from the audience, they seemed like a bunch of friends playing at a party.

I was thrilled by the performance and so was the rest of the audience. The atmosphere was fantastic and everyone was dancing and smiling. It felt like a special occasion, and we were the only people involved in it. It was a very memorable experience for me and it confirmed for me that The Highlights are my favourite band of all time!

QUESTION 4 *Task specific mark scheme*

Content
The essay must fully address the points made in the statement – that everyone should travel abroad and that travelling abroad is something 'essential'. The writer can totally agree or disagree, or both agree and disagree. The writer's opinions must be supported by logical arguments and reasons.

Range of grammar and vocabulary
A wide variety of verb tenses should be used accurately, for example present tenses for general and current situations, and past simple and present perfect tenses for past situations and facts. Conditional structures, relative clauses and passive structures may also be required. Structures and vocabulary for giving opinions must be used accurately, and vocabulary connected with travel, advantages and disadvantages, and feelings and attitudes should also be used accurately.

Register

The register should be neutral or fairly formal. The topic is a fairly serious one and an essay should not be too informal.

Organization and cohesion

The essay should begin and end with a brief introduction and conclusion. Between those, it should be appropriately divided into paragraphs, each of which deals with a different aspect of the topic. Different paragraphs may agree or disagree with the statement. Points should be linked with reasons and arguments supporting them by the accurate use of linking words and phrases. Appropriate linking words and phrases should also be used for moving from one point to another.

Target reader

The reader should understand fully the writer's views on the topic, and the arguments that the writer puts forward in support of those views.

Model answer ESSEY

Of course, these days travelling abroad is commonplace, and a considerable number of people have experience of it. Many young people go travelling for quite long periods when they are students, lots of people have holidays abroad, and many schools organize trips for schoolchildren. It is generally assumed that going to other countries is a good thing, but whether or not it is 'essential' is another matter.

This assumes that people who have never been to another country are in some way missing something, that their lives are in some way incomplete because of this. I am not convinced that this is the case. I think it is quite possible to learn a lot about life, and to have an enormous variety of experiences of life, if you stay in your own country for the whole of your life. That is of course what previous generations did, when there was little or no opportunity for foreign travel. We cannot say that people today who have travelled abroad are automatically 'better' in some way than everyone from the past.

It is also debatable whether everyone who does travel abroad today can be said to benefit from the experience in any serious way. Lots of people who go abroad are not really interested in the places they visit, and make no effort to learn anything about the culture, the people, the history or the way of life in the places they visit.

So I do not believe that travelling abroad is 'essential'. Of course, it is a great experience for many people, but I don't think it is necessarily something that everyone must do.

Paper 3: Use of English

PART 1

1	C	5	A	9	A
2	A	6	D	10	C
3	B	7	B	11	B
4	D	8	C	12	D

PART 2

13	the	21	took
14	such	22	in
15	of	23	These / Those / They
16	were	24	Had
17	to	25	which
18	for	26	no
19	as	27	being
20	other		

PART 3

28	network	33	emission
29	length	34	partnership
30	convenience	35	replace
31	beneficial	36	efficiency
32	easing	37	developers

PART 4

38	clear	41	good
39	see	42	relate
40	interest		

PART 5

43 haven't / have not got **round**][to answering
44 of][no **use**
45 **do you feel** like][having something
46 was a **matter**][of minutes
47 no **doubt** (that)][things will get
48 was Jake who / that][**got** me interested
49 was **desperate** to][give
50 injury][**prevented** him from playing

Paper 4: Listening

PART 1

1	B	4	A
2	B	5	B
3	B	6	C

PART 2

7	construction business	11	marketing ideas
8	don't(-)wants	12	physical distractions
9	road map	13	past
10	time management	14	problem(-)solvers

PART 3

15 B	18 C
16 C	19 C
17 A	20 B

PART 4

21 D	25 C	29 A
22 A	26 D	30 C
23 G	27 H	
24 F	28 F	

Paper 5: Speaking

Teachers should use their own judgement to award marks out of 20 based on the assessment criteria on page 103.

TEST 4

Paper 1: Reading

PART 1

1 A	4 C
2 B	5 C
3 A	6 A

PART 2

7 C	10 B
8 D	11 F
9 G	12 E

PART 3

13 A	17 C
14 B	18 A
15 A	19 A
16 D	

PART 4

20 B	25 C	30 A
21 D	26 C	31 C
22 E	27 D	32 B
23 D	28 A	33 B
24 D	29 E	34 E

Paper 2: Writing

For General impression mark scheme, see page 102.

QUESTION 1 *Task specific mark scheme*

Content

The proposal should present a coherent programme for the day, using the list of suggestions made in the meeting and the list of notes made by the writer. It is not necessary to use everything in the lists, and it may not be possible to do so without making the proposal too long. Items from the lists should be selected in order to create a proposed programme for the day that makes sense.

Range of grammar and vocabulary

The accurate use of modals such as *would*, *could* and *should* is required, as is the accurate use of other structures for making suggestions and recommendations. Future verb tenses may also be required. Vocabulary for describing the various activities and items on the programme must be used accurately.

Register

The register should be fairly formal or neutral, as is appropriate for the subject matter of the proposal.

Organization and cohesion

The proposal should be appropriately divided into paragraphs or sections, each dealing with separate parts of the programme or a separate part of the day. The proposal may have an overall heading. The various parts of the programme should be linked with appropriate linking words and phrases, and items on the proposed programme should be appropriately linked with reasons for including them.

Target reader

The reader should be absolutely clear about what the proposed programme would include, when each item would happen and what each item would involve.

Model answer

PROPOSED SCHEDULE FOR VISITORS, 26 JUNE

The day should begin, as suggested in the meeting, with the visitors being welcomed in the reception area. I suggest that Laura should give a short welcoming speech – as Head of Human Resources, she's done the same kind of thing quite often in the past.

Following that, I think we should divide them into groups of four for the tour of the building. This would mean three small groups – I could take one, Laura could take one and Simon could take the other. We should keep the tour to a maximum of about 30 minutes and then we should all gather together in the Conference Room. We can have coffee there, and then I suggest that Charles comes to give a talk about our activities. We can then go to the Executive Suite for lunch. I think that all the Heads of Department should join us for lunch.

After lunch, I think that we should take them to watch us doing what we normally do. I think this would be much better than the talk suggested at the meeting. To see us in action will be more interesting for them.

I think we could end the day with a Question and Answer session, which I'm happy to conduct. We could then give them an information pack and a 'bag of goodies' of the kind we usually give to visitors.

QUESTION 2 *Task specific mark scheme*

Content

The letter must include reference to all the matters mentioned in the advertisement – why the writer wishes to work at the festival, what job the writer would like to get and why they prefer this, and reasons why the writer is suitable for the job. There should also be a reference to the writer's ability at English. A second choice of job may also be given.

Range of grammar and vocabulary

A variety of verb tenses must be used accurately – present for the writer's qualities and current situation, past for the writer's background and future for the writer's plans and hopes. It is likely that the present perfect tense will be required. Vocabulary connected with the situation and the type of work must be used accurately, as should words and phrases that are appropriate for a letter of application.

Register

The letter should be fairly formal but polite and friendly – it is a job application for temporary work in informal surroundings. The letter should also indicate the writer's enthusiasm for the job.

Organization and cohesion

The letter should begin with an appropriate introduction and end with an appropriate ending for a job application. It should be appropriately divided into paragraphs dealing with why the writer wants to work at the festival, the job preferred, the writer's background and experience and reasons why the writer is suitable for the job. Sentences and paragraphs should be appropriately linked.

Target reader

The reader should understand fully why the writer is applying, what job the writer prefers and why, and why the writer believes he/she is suitable for that job.

Model answer

Dear Sir / Madam,

I am writing to apply for work at your festival this summer. I would particularly like to work on one of the stalls selling merchandise for the artists appearing.

I have been to several major rock festivals in my own country as a member of the audience and I have also previously worked on two occasions on stalls at a festival. Your festival is well-known in many other countries, including mine, and I would really welcome the opportunity to work at it. I am planning to travel round Britain during the summer and the experience of working at your festival while I am in Britain would be fantastic for me.

My level of English is very good (please see the attached list of my qualifications and previous experience). I very much enjoy meeting people and I feel that I would be suited

to working on a stall and dealing with members of the audience. I am also quite knowledgeable about many of the artists who will be appearing at the festival, and this will be an advantage when selling their merchandise on the stall. My previous experience at festivals has included of course handling money and also dealing efficiently with large queues of customers.

I hope that you will be able to offer me work at your festival. Should you be unable to use me on a merchandise stall, I would also be more than willing to work in catering, selling food on a stall or in a tent.

I look forward to hearing from you.

Yours faithfully

QUESTION 3 *Task specific mark scheme*

Content

The research project contribution must fully address all the matters mentioned in the question. It must refer both to the young people who do further studies after school and to those who go straight into employment.

Range of grammar and vocabulary

It is likely that the present continuous tense and the present perfect tense are required and these must be used appropriately. Appropriate past tenses may be required for comparisons with the past. Comparative structures are also required to talk about changes. Appropriate vocabulary for education and employment must be used accurately. Vocabulary connected with increases and decreases and with changes must also be used accurately.

Register

The register should be fairly formal or neutral, as is appropriate for a piece of research on a serious topic, involving facts.

Organization and cohesion

The research project contribution should be appropriately divided into paragraphs. This may involve a short introductory paragraph about the area of research, and separate paragraphs about the two different aspects (further studies and work). There may be a brief closing paragraph providing a short summary. Appropriate linking words and phrases should be used throughout, for example for a list of points (*Firstly, Secondly*).

Target reader

The reader should have a clear understanding of the situation regarding school leavers in that place, and what they currently do after leaving school.

Model answer   *contribution*

The question of what young people do after they leave school in this part of the country is one that has been addressed by a series of surveys carried out by various organizations. These surveys reveal a fast-changing situation.

The surveys show that an increasing number of young people are going from school into further education rather than straight into employment. The figure for those doing further studies has risen by 35% compared with five years ago. This is a significant rise, and reflects both the fact that more young people now want to get further educational qualifications that they feel will be to their advantage in the world of work, and the fact that the provision of further education in the region has risen significantly. Eight new colleges have opened over the past ten years and many others have expanded.

The surveys also indicate that there have been significant changes concerning those young people who go directly from school into employment. Firstly, an increasing number are leaving the rural areas and going to work in the towns and cities – the figure for people doing that has gone up 15% compared with five years ago and 56% compared with ten years ago. Secondly, there is a pattern of young people being employed in the service industries rather than in the industrial or manufacturing sectors. Ten years ago, 67% of all school leavers going directly into employment were employed in manufacturing or manual work. That figure is now down to 28%.

QUESTION 4 *Task specific mark scheme*

Content

The competition entry must explain who the chosen person is, why the writer has chosen that person, why the writer would like to spend a day with that person and what would happen on the day.

Range of grammar and vocabulary

It is likely that modals such as *would* are required to talk about this hypothetical situation, and conditional structures may also be required. Vocabulary describing people's personalities must be used accurately, and vocabulary associated with the chosen person's job / life is also required.

Register

The register should be fairly informal – the competition is asking for personal preferences and feelings about a topic / hypothetical situation that is not very serious.

Organization and cohesion

The competition entry should be appropriately divided into paragraphs, with perhaps separate paragraphs dealing with the person and why the writer wants to spend a day with him/her, followed by the writers' ideas for how the day would be spent. Different events on the day should be linked with appropriate linking words and phrases, and the writer's preferences should be appropriately linked with the reasons for them.

Target reader

The reader should fully understand who the chosen person is, why the writer has chosen that person, and what would happen on the day the writer spent with that person.

Model answer

THE PERSON I'D MOST LIKE TO SPEND A DAY WITH

The person I would most like to spend a day with is the footballer Harry Vincent. He plays for the club I support and for the national team, and he's one of the most famous people in this country at the moment. He seems from the outside to be someone who can handle all the pressure of being a top sportsman and all the attention that comes with it in a very calm way. He seems like a pleasant person who hasn't let it all go to his head and who remains 'himself' despite all the things that have happened to him.

I'd like to spend a day with him because I'd like to find out what it's like to be a top professional footballer and what it's like to be a celebrity at the same time. I'd like the day to be a day when the national team is playing and I'd like to experience that day from his point of view. I'd meet up with him at the beginning of the day and then see what happens when the team gets together before a game. I'd find out what it's like behind the scenes of a big game, and how he and the other players react to the result of the game. Then I'd see what happens afterwards, with all the interviews and all the inevitable questions about his private life. I've seen all this on TV – it would be fascinating to experience it all first-hand and find out whether he really is the way he seems.

Paper 3: Use of English

PART 1

1 C	5 B	9 B
2 B	6 A	10 A
3 D	7 D	11 C
4 C	8 A	12 B

PART 2

13 to
14 There
15 into
16 part
17 so
18 As
19 towards
20 of
21 because
22 well
23 get
24 for
25 have / include
26 a
27 with

PART 3

28 originally	33 work(-)out
29 existence	34 necessarily
30 minority	35 maximize / maximise
31 sight	36 strengthening
32 untrained	37 entirety

PART 4

38 settled	41 contact
39 part	42 drop
40 fine	

PART 5

43 **come** up with][a solution
44 be wondering why][it **has** been
45 me of not][telling the **truth**
46 **without** giving][enough thought
47 there has been][a **decrease** in
48 **however** bad][his behaviour OR
   however badly(-)behaved][he
49 **only** I][hadn't made
50 **accounts** for][the difference

Paper 4: Listening

PART 1

1 B	4 B
2 A	5 A
3 C	6 A

PART 2

7 (the) S/scissor M/man
8 scholars
9 alphabet
10 illustrations
11 moral lessons
12 toys
13 common themes
14 innocent

PART 3

15 D	18 C
16 B	19 C
17 A	20 A

PART 4

21 E	25 D	29 B
22 B	26 D	30 A
23 G	27 G	
24 C	28 F	

Paper 5: Speaking

Teachers should use their own judgement to award marks out of 20 based on the assessment criteria on page 103.

TEST 1

Part One.
You will hear three different extracts. For questions 1–6, choose the answer (A, B or C) which fits best according to what you hear. There are two questions for each extract.

ONE.
You hear two people talking about public speaking.

Woman: I dread the experience. It's the anticipation that gets me. Once I start I'm usually OK but beforehand I panic. I think that my mind will go blank and everyone will stare at me. This happened once. I was trying to speak and listen to my own voice at the same time but all I could hear was silence. I seemed to have forgotten how to speak and I felt my face go red. I fumbled for my notes and simply read out the rest of the speech.

Man: Well, fear of public speaking, or what is called 'pre-presentational anxiety', is normal. If you think about it, public speaking is not a natural thing to do. You don't want to humiliate yourself in front of people. But with preparation and practice, even the most stressed public speakers can conquer their fears. There are very few people who are quick, intelligent and extrovert enough to just get up and deliver something spontaneously. If you're giving a speech, you must carefully plan what you're going to say.

Woman: I find it also helps not to think of yourself the whole time. Once you shift the focus on to the people you are speaking to, you feel the pressure lift.

repeat extract 1

TWO.
You hear part of a radio programme about the London Underground.

Man: As part of a huge publicity drive in the 1920s and 1930s, London Transport launched a poster campaign to persuade people to move into the suburbs and make use of the rapidly expanding Underground network. Tell us about that, Zoe.

Woman: Well, the posters were used to encourage people to live in and enjoy the quiet and domestic life of the suburbs and travel into London for work and leisure. They helped to shape people's perceptions and expectations of London and what it meant to live there in a period of great change. As well as persuading people to move out to the suburbs, there was a drive for people to make use of the city at a time when the leisure industry was expanding.

Man: What kind of things did these posters show?

Woman: Well, despite the fact that many women worked in the 1920s and 1930s, the posters depicted a domestic ideal, with pictures of women playing with their children in the park and preparing meals for their husbands' return. More and more people were becoming middle class and part of this ideal was that the husband would go to work and the wife would stay at home, even though this was not the case for many families.

repeat extract 2

THREE.
You hear two people discussing the news media.

Man: Of course, the cliché is 'don't believe everything you read in the papers', and I guess there's some truth in that. But in many ways that's not backed up by the evidence. Look at all the times when stories would never have come out if it hadn't been for the much-maligned news media.

Woman: I don't know about that. Personally I'm always pretty sceptical when it comes to all these revelations. I mean, look at medical stories. It sometimes seems as if every day brings some new health scare – you mustn't eat that, you should drink that – and most of these things you never hear about again. I think it'd be really interesting to find out how many of these stories actually turn out to be true. I reckon they just write these things to create a stir. I mean, lots of them are in the entertainment industry really, aren't they? 'Don't let the facts get in the way of a good story' is the joke in the trade isn't it? I think lots of them live by that.

Man: I don't think that's really fair. There are lots of investigative journalists who've done the public a great service by exposing things they otherwise would never have known about.

repeat extract 3
That is the end of Part 1.

Now turn to Part 2.
You will hear part of a talk about the invention of the microwave oven. For questions 7–14, complete the sentences.
You now have 45 seconds to look at Part 2.

Man: One day in spring 1945, physics engineer Percy Spencer was walking past a switched-on piece of radar equipment when he felt something sticky in his pocket. It turned out to be a chocolate peanut bar he had been saving for his coffee break. Intrigued, he set out to discover why it had suddenly melted. The equipment concerned was a magnetron tube – the heart of a radar set. Radar had been invented by the British in World War II to detect enemy aircraft at night using short waves, or microwaves. But it wasn't until Spencer, an engineer at a small-time firm called Raytheon in Boston, US, worked out a way of mass-producing the tubes, that radar made a real difference in the war.

The day after the chocolate incident, Spencer

sent a boy out to buy some popcorn. He placed the kernels near the magnetron tube. They immediately started popping round the lab. His next experiment was with an egg, which he put inside a kettle. Curious colleagues gathered round to watch it quaking – one unlucky director bent down to take a closer look just at the moment the egg exploded. Spencer came to realize that the microwaves were heating the food by agitating its water and fat molecules, which meant that the inside cooked just as fast as the outside. Raytheon engineers soon refined the idea: the first microwave, 5ft 6in tall and weighing 750lb, was installed in a Boston restaurant for testing in 1946.

The first commercial microwave hit the market the following year. It was named Radarange following a competition among Raytheon employees. Spencer and his colleagues confidently expected a cooking revolution. But the machine was primitive, enormous and, at $3,000, too expensive. All too soon, chefs realized its main drawback: meat refused to brown and food emerged limp and flabby. The company chairman's chef quit in disgust because he was told to use the Radarange. Not until the 1960s, when the first counter-top microwave was produced, did sales at last begin to take off. The first model in 1967 was 100 volts and cost just under $500. By 1975, sales of microwaves overtook gas cookers in the US. Now, nearly 90% of households in Britain and the US use a microwave oven.

Now you will hear Part 2 again.
repeat Part 2
That is the end of Part 2.

Now turn to Part 3.
You will hear a radio interview with someone who has been having ballet lessons. For questions 15–20, choose the answer (A, B, C or D) which fits best according to what you hear.
You now have 1 minute to look at Part 3.

Interviewer: Today I'm talking to opera critic Rupert Christiansen, who is in his forties and has recently started doing ballet classes. It's a pretty unusual thing to do, isn't it?

Rupert: Well, yes, but one consolation of growing old is that you cease to care what other people think of your views or activities. So here I am, coming out on the radio as probably the only balding middle-aged man on the entire planet to take up ballet lessons. Go on, snigger.

Interviewer: I'm not laughing, I'm just interested. Tell me, how did it all start?

Rupert: Well, I have long been an infatuated ballet fan. The way most men think about their football team, I think about the Royal Ballet company– they're my team and I follow their every move with nerdy fascination.

Recently, I've become increasingly frustrated at my lack of technical knowledge, but the thought of having a bash myself hadn't crossed my mind since a schoolboy attempt at ballroom dancing culminated in disaster. Anyway, many years after that unfortunate event, to stave off bodily decay, I discovered Balance, a wonderful physiotherapy gym in London, where I began personal training with Hans Ektvedt and his colleagues. Hans nobly takes me through the necessary boring stuff – weights, pull-ups, crunches – and his patience and good humour make it endurable and almost enjoyable.

Interviewer: So what led you from that to ballet lessons?

Rupert: One day earlier this year, Hans mentioned a newcomer to the Balance team and suggested I try him for some supplementary lessons. His name is Julien Diaz, and he turns out to be a remarkable character. A graduate of the Rambert Dance School, he ended up dancing professionally in Berlin and Amsterdam, before returning to England to set up as a trainer, specializing in posture and the freeing up of body language. He told me I should start doing ballet and his disarming manner soon persuaded me to drop my inhibitions. I was under no illusions about my abilities but I wanted to find out about the art of ballet by trying it myself.

Interviewer: Isn't it a bit dangerous for someone of your age, if you don't mind me saying so?

Rupert: Well, as Julien says, it's a superb form of exercise. He'd like to see the whole world doing ballet. It's only dangerous to muscles if you do it day in, day out at the very top level. For almost anyone else, it's an injury-preventative activity that tones and elongates every part of your body, from toes to fingers to head. It's a training in balance, co-ordination and flexibility, which gets you to engage your body and brain at the same time. It's fantastic for getting you to walk with a spring in your step, and it also cleanses the mind – there's no way you can do a ballet class without concentrating 100 per cent on what you're doing.

Interviewer: So what do your lessons consist of?

Rupert: The sessions last for 90 minutes. We start with what are basically bending and stretching exercises. Then we move on to the hopping, skipping and turning movements, finishing with some jumps in both the closed first and open second positions, before cooling down with some excruciating but vital stretches. This is basic stuff, but, believe me, it isn't easy, and you have to take it slowly. I'm not unfit, but I can't do more than a couple of minutes without gasping for rest, and it's incredibly difficult to programme it all into one's muscle memory. You can't approximate – you have to get it right, and that involves focusing simultaneously on the correct angle of turnout, the complementary shaping of the arms, a firm finish to any sequence of movements, and the fluent placing of the head, neck and shoulders.

Interviewer: Are you going to get really good at this? What kind of progress are you hoping to make?

Rupert: How much further can I get? Well, I'm not expecting a call from by beloved Royal Ballet. My main aim is to find out something of what it feels like to dance, from the inside – already I find that, as a spectator, my admiration for the professionals has sharpened considerably. Julien has a potty notion of moulding some of the movements I am painfully acquiring into a dance, and believes that most people of my age could reach a point at which they could take the lower grades of Royal Academy of Dance exams. And Hans has noticed that my work with Julien has resulted in improvements in my regular training. He says that I'm moving better and walking taller, with firmer core stability and more flexibility in my hips and back. I wonder whether he's tempted to have a go himself.

Interviewer: So presumably, you would recommend ballet lessons ...

Now you will hear Part 3 again.
repeat Part 3
That is the end of Part 3.

Now turn to Part 4.
Part 4 consists of two tasks. You will hear five short extracts in which people are talking about people they know. Look at Task 1. For questions 21–25, choose from the list A–H the description each speaker gives of the person. Now look at Task 2. For questions 26–30, choose from the list A–H the feeling each speaker expresses about the person. While you listen you must complete both tasks.
You now have 45 seconds to look at Part 4.

Speaker 1 I know people say he thinks a lot of himself, and, well, they've got a point, he certainly isn't what you'd call modest. He'll be the first one to tell you how brilliant he is and how hard he's worked and you certainly couldn't accuse him of lacking confidence. Quite frankly, a lot of people think he's an absolute pain and steer clear of him, because he's always going on about himself. Anything you've done, he can top it. But the fact is, I know another side of him, the kind side that means he'll do anything for a friend. And he's done me a lot of big favours so I stand by him. When other people have a go at him, I always defend him.

Speaker 2 She's certainly had a lot of knocks in her life but she keeps bouncing back. She's definitely what you'd call resilient, and all these terrible things that have happened, she just seems to take them in her stride, and hardly talks about them. I wish I could be like that – I always seem to cave in at the slightest hint of trouble, I don't seem to be able to just get on with life when something goes wrong. But she's got this incredible strength that keeps her going – it must be great to be like that. She doesn't want anyone feeling pity for her – she hates that and she doesn't need it.

Speaker 3 You never know what's going to happen with him, because he's never the same. One time you're with him he's cheerful and sociable, the next time he sits quietly in the corner and doesn't want to speak to anyone. Some people find that very hard to handle and he often loses friends because of it. I think that might well happen with me because, to be honest, it gets on my nerves. You want your friends to be basically the same most of the time, not always up and down like he is. I know it's not the nicest thing to say, but sometimes I just want to yell at him.

Speaker 4 He's one of those people who's always finding fault with things – nothing's ever good enough for him, there's always something wrong. He likes nothing better than to moan, and my goodness, can he moan? You've never heard anything like him when he gets going. People wonder why I spend so much time with him, considering that he's always like that, but the fact is I find it hilarious. Once he gets going, it's as much as I can do to keep a straight face. And, believe it or not, he sees the funny side sometimes. He's not as serious about everything as most people think he is.

Speaker 5 You never know whether you can take what he tells you at face value or not because he makes a lot of it up. He'll tell you he's doing one thing when in fact he's doing another and he tells different people different things. I sometimes wonder if he can remember all the different versions he's given! He's always up to something – covering up something he shouldn't have done, or coming up with some cunning plan. To be honest, I feel sorry for him, it must be terrible to spend your whole life pretending. He must be very unhappy at heart and I wouldn't wish that on anyone.

Now you will hear Part 4 again.
repeat Part 4
That is the end of Part 4.
That is the end of the test.

TEST 2

Part One
You will hear three different extracts. For questions 1–6, choose the answer (A, B or C) which fits best according to what you hear. There are two questions for each extract.

ONE.

You hear part of a radio programme about a famous London hotel.

Presenter: Tea at the Grand Hotel in London is served in the Green Room, a light, airy space with luxuriant plants, fountains and a panoramic view over the city. Dress is strictly smart-casual. There are four sittings for tea, the first at 11.30 in the morning and the last at 6.30 in the evening. Despite the high price tag, tables are booked up months in advance. Tea includes a selection of sandwiches – crustless of course – scones, cakes and pastries. There are 12 types of tea on offer, including the Grand's own superior afternoon brew. David James has been manager of the Green Room for 15 years. David, tea at the Grand is very popular, isn't it?

Hotel manager: Yes, indeed. When I first started, we had 80 to 100 people a day. Now it's twice that number.

Presenter: And are they all wealthy people?

Hotel manager: Not at all. I can tell as soon as someone walks in what type of person they are, where they are from, why they are here. Some people who come here have lots of money and some don't. When someone has saved to come here as a treat, I like to make a special effort to make them feel comfortable.

repeat extract 1

TWO.

You hear two presenters talking on a science programme.

Woman: Possibly one of the most talked about pieces of research recently published has surprisingly little to do with anything of particular importance. Entitled 'The Case of the Disappearing Teaspoons', the study proves that this is a naturally occurring phenomenon with no apparent explanation.

Man: Yes, a research team in Australia placed 70 numbered teaspoons in various tea-rooms at their Institute and tracked them over a period of five months. Eighty per cent disappeared for good. It was calculated that they had a half-life – that is, the length of time it took for half of the teaspoons to disappear – of 81 days. If this is a global phenomenon, then 600,000 teaspoons are disappearing each year.

Woman: So where have they all gone? Practical and mundane explanations include people taking them home or losing them under piles of work. However, with such a large quantity of teaspoons being lost each year, many people feel these explanations are simply not sufficient.

repeat extract 2

THREE.

You hear two people talking about popular music.

Woman: One thing that's quite interesting about popular music is how derivative and imitative it is. You see, most of the innovations that took place in it had happened by the end of the 1970s, and after that it's all been copies of what had already been and gone.

Man: That's just not true. There's lots of really innovative new music going on now and there always will be. Every new generation develops its own styles and sounds that are unique to it.

Woman: No, they just think that's what they're doing. Actually, they're just recycling old things. Granted, they sometimes do that very well, but it's all been done before. The truth is, it's new for them but it's not actually new.

Man: But the fans, the public, they don't see it that way do they?

Woman: No, they buy the music and they go to concerts by the latest successful or fashionable bands and singers and they think it's all being done for the first time. It's only older people like me who spot the similarities with music from the past. Like a lot of things, influences pass from one generation to another, and it's not always a conscious thing.

repeat extract 3
That is the end of Part 1.

Now turn to Part 2.
You will hear part of a talk about a common psychological phenomenon.
For questions 7–14, complete the sentences.
You now have 45 seconds to look at Part 2.

Woman: Have you ever had the feeling that something that happens has happened before? Have you had an experience that seems very familiar, and felt that you've been through it before? This phenomenon is known as déjà vu, which is French for 'already seen'. But it doesn't tend to be unusual events that trigger the feeling. Psychologists say that it is usually life's more mundane details – the click of a radiator, the movement of the shadows on a tablecloth – that prompt this sudden and sometimes breathtaking sense of familiarity. And new research has opened a promising window on the phenomenon, providing both possible explanations for the sensation and novel ways to create and measure it.

In surveys, about two-thirds of adults report having had at least one déjà vu experience, and the sensation seems to occur most often in people with lively imaginations. People who travel a lot are more likely to report the experiences than homebodies, and those with advanced degrees report having it more often than others. Rates seem to peak in young adulthood and to fall off gradually through retirement age, when many people live daily routines that really are familiar.

Researchers at Duke University in North Carolina and Southern Methodist University in Texas, USA have tried to produce in the laboratory a feeling that is close to the kind of unexplained familiarity people know in life. In a series of experiments, they had college students examine photographs, trying to locate a small black or white cross. The pictures included scenes at Duke University, such as the chapel, and buildings at Southern Methodist University. A week later, the students returned to examine the photos again, but this time they had different backgrounds. The students were asked to say whether they had ever been to the places shown.

The expectation was that while the students focused on the crosses, the photos would imprint on their memories unconsciously, leaving impressions that later seemed familiar. And in the first session of 81 students, the predictions proved true. Duke students who had never been to Southern Methodist said they believed they had been to the campus in the photos taken at Southern Methodist; many Southern Methodist students said they thought they had been to the campus in photos taken at Duke, when they had not.

Now you will hear Part 2 again.
repeat Part 2
That is the end of Part 2.

Now turn to Part 3.
You will hear a radio discussion about writing a novel.
For questions 15–20, choose the answer (A, B, C or D) which fits best according to what you hear.
You now have 1 minute to look at Part 3.

Interviewer: OK, in our weekly spot about how to write a novel, I'm talking to novelist Louise Doughty. Louise, this week we're talking about getting comments and feedback on your work from other people. 'If there is anything in your own work you think particularly fine,' said Ernest Hemingway, 'strike it out.' Is that good advice?

Novelist: Well, few would-be novelists aspire to be as plain and brutal as Hemingway, I suspect, but his dictum is still worth tucking into a corner of your brain – not to be followed slavishly, but as an antidote to that great curse of the inexperienced novelist: over-writing.

Interviewer: How do you know if you are over-writing?

Novelist: Well, an excess of adverbs and adjectives is a clue. Repetition under the guise of emphasis is another, and extended metaphors should be rationed tightly.

Interviewer: Now, there comes a point in the writing of every novel when you just don't know any more. You've been immersed in it for weeks, possibly years. You've lost sight of the original impetus behind the book and are plagued with self-doubt – yet at the same time you know there is something there and are not ready to give up on it.

Novelist: Yes, and this is the point at which you should be getting feedback.

Interviewer: From whom?

Novelist: As a rule, I'd advise against getting it from your nearest and dearest. You will be wounded by their criticism and suspicious of their praise. Instead, join a writing a community of some sort. You need comments from another writer. Those who have been logging onto my website will know that such a community has formed there. Creative writing courses and book groups are also good places to find like-minded souls. Through such contacts you can find someone who understands what you are trying to do – which is not the same as someone who is uncritical of the way you do it. There is a time and a place for emotional support, but that is not what we are talking about here.

Interviewer: What kind of comments are useful in your view?

Novelist: Well, you need someone who is prepared to say, 'I really like the opening paragraph but I thought it went a bit wrong after that because ...' and, crucially, is prepared to be specific. 'I just didn't like him' is not a helpful comment on a character. 'I lost sympathy with him in the scene where he tells his brother the truth because I thought he was too brutal. Maybe you should re-write it making his motivation clearer and his language softer.' That is useful advice: you can choose whether to take it or discard it. Similarly, at the level of prose style, some well-meaning person might say 'It's a bit boring', but a helpful critic would say 'You have three paragraphs of description here before you tell us who is talking; maybe you should consider starting the conversation first and weaving all the description in, instead of having it all in one chunk.'

Interviewer: How do you personally get feedback on your work?

Novelist: The most fruitful relationships I have with other writers are with the novelists with whom I swap work – usually the person whose novel is under discussion pays for dinner. If you can find other novelists who are working at a similar level to yourself, with similar interests, and who are frank and unafraid of frankness from you, then keep them close at hand.

Interviewer: Now what about reactions to feedback? We've talked about getting it, but what about when you've got it?

Novelist: Well, even with a trusted ally, there comes a point when you have to stick to your guns and say, 'This person whom I really respect doesn't like this bit but I do and it's staying in.' And of course, feedback can be annoying. For a start, a lot of the criticism you receive will be stuff which you knew already in your heart of hearts – you were just hoping nobody else would notice. And sometimes, you will bristle at a certain comment on your work, not because it is untrue but because the consequences of righting that particular defect are too daunting to contemplate at that particular time – accurate criticism is the most painful of all. On other occasions, you will have a gut feeling that the person reading your work just doesn't 'get' it, or wants you to write a different novel entirely. Frequently, the only way to work out if criticism is useful is to nod sagely, then file it in a drawer. When the wounds have healed over and your ego is not under immediate threat, then you will be able to assess its true worth.

Interviewer: Right. Now let's move on to talk about ...

Now you will hear Part 3 again.
repeat Part 3
That is the end of Part 3.

Now turn to Part 4.
Part 4 consists of two tasks. You will hear five short extracts in which people are talking about events they attended. Look at Task 1. For questions 21–25, choose from the list A–H the event each person is talking about. Now look at Task 2. For questions 26–30, choose from the list A–H what happened according to each speaker. While you listen you must complete both tasks. You now have 45 seconds to look at Part 4.

Speaker 1 It certainly wasn't like any other I've been to, and I've been to a few. There was a strange atmosphere as everyone gathered and I thought there was a definite tension in the air. Everyone was clearly divided into two sides and there was clearly some history between them. Anyway, the main part passed off OK, and I was having a decent time, chatting to all sorts of people. Then, all of a sudden, one group was shouting at each other and pointing fingers and generally being very unpleasant. It was quite a scene and insults were exchanged. Fortunately, I don't think the happy couple saw any of it, so I don't think it spoilt their day.

Speaker 2 There was certainly a big turnout, more than I'd expected. I hadn't been very sure about whether to go or not, I don't normally like that kind of thing. I thought it would all be ultra-competitive, with everyone trying to prove they'd done better than everyone else since we last met. But actually, we all got on famously and had a great time reminiscing about the old days. Even the people I hadn't liked much before were good company. It was a shame when it ended, I'd have liked to talk to them for longer. I wrote down lots of addresses and phone numbers and we all agreed to keep in touch, though I don't know if we will.

Speaker 3 It wasn't the best organized thing I've ever been to. They should have kept it down to just a few key people, instead of which the place was crammed with all sorts of people that didn't have much to do with the matter at hand. It became apparent pretty quickly that very little was going to be achieved. Half the people couldn't hear what the other half were saying and we didn't even get through the first point for discussion. So the people in charge decided to cut it short and call another one, with fewer people, some time later. So we were all back outside ages before it was supposed to finish. It was a farce, really.

Speaker 4 I turned up because I used to work with both of them, though I hadn't seen either of them for quite some time. Our career paths had gone in different directions. Actually, it was a bit of a shame, because they'd gone to a lot of trouble to organize it and then half the people they were expecting didn't turn up. They'd both given years of good service, you'd have thought more people would have shown up for their last day, but I guess they couldn't be bothered. I'd only been planning to stay for a short while, but I hung on till the end. I didn't have the heart to go, they looked so disappointed.

Speaker 5 It was quite a performance getting there – all sorts of traffic jams – so I missed the beginning. There was only one empty seat when I got in there, so I just had to sit in it. When I looked round at one point, I realized I was sitting next to a neighbour I've never been able to stand. This put me off a bit, because I've always avoided him and I didn't want to end up having to talk to him when the thing was over. I was thinking more about that than what the kids were doing up there. What I did listen to sounded pretty good, and I knew they'd been rehearsing for ages. Anyway, as soon as the last bit was over, I just rushed for the door and got out of there.

Now you will hear Part 4 again.
repeat Part 4
That is the end of Part 4.
That is the end of the test.

TEST 3

Part One
You will hear three different extracts. For questions 1–6, choose the answer (A, B or C) which fits best according to what you hear. There are two questions for each extract.

ONE.
You hear two people talking about reading books aloud for children.

Man: I'm a terrible ham when it comes to reading to my kids. I like to do all the voices so I look for books with lots of dialogue and different characters. My kids are totally unimpressed and probably prefer having their mother read to them. She reads in a very soothing voice, and she's not trying to act or show off. It reminds me of listening to my own mother read when I was a kid.

Woman: Yes, I always claim that I read aloud to our three children for their benefit. That it's good for their educational development to sit and listen last thing at night. That somehow, through hearing a story, their creative juices will be stirred. But it is, of course, for me. Nothing can beat the delight of disappearing into a new thrilling chapter. And I bet I'm not the only parent who, having turned out the light and said goodnight to their grateful offspring, sits down on the stairs and reads on to find out what happens next.

repeat extract 1

TWO.
You hear part of a radio programme.

Presenter: Statistics on how many people go into business with their friends are hard to come by, but it's one of the most popular ways for individuals to start businesses. If you have a passion, a great idea for a business, you're not inclined to talk to strangers about it. You might also be one of those people that think they don't have the skills to start the business alone and want some complementary capabilities or expertise. And many people turn to a friend for that. But such partnerships are fraught with danger, as Matt Lauzon discovered when he set one up with a friend. Matt, what happened?

Man: Well, we both underestimated the time and effort it would take to get the business off the ground. We made a deal when we started that we'd have a 50-50 partnership, but I felt I was doing 90 per cent of the work. I didn't have the heart to tell my partner he was not holding up his end of the bargain, so we ended up breaking up the business because we weren't getting anywhere. It's very difficult to manage people but even more difficult to manage friends. It's hard to delegate who will do what. The business collapsed but I'm happy with the way things turned out, because the friendship survived.

repeat extract 2

THREE.
You hear two people on a radio programme talking about running.

Man: Some people think there's only one way to become a better runner – and that's to run. But I'd argue that by confining your sessions purely to running, you are missing out on lots of fitness attributes that could contribute to improving your technique, your running economy – that's your ability to run faster without using up more energy – and your injury resistance.

Woman: Absolutely. Running is a perfectly natural activity but the body was designed to move in all directions, using a variety of muscle groups, not just in a forward direction using only the lower body, often on unforgiving, hard surfaces. If running is all you do, some muscle groups get flabby and lazy through under-use, while others become tight and short through overuse. If you can strengthen the neglected muscles, stretch the tight ones and make the most heavily used ones more resilient, you'll be on the way to a more balanced body and this will translate into better running. And by better, I don't just mean faster – I mean more comortable, less strained and altogether more enjoyable.

repeat extract 3
That is the end of Part 1.

Now turn to Part 2.
You will hear someone who works as a life coach talking about her work. For questions 7–14, complete the sentences.
You now have 45 seconds to look at Part 2.

Woman: I am standing in the middle of a group of people at an event and someone asks the inevitable question 'What do you do?' When I say that I am a Life Coach I often encounter a puzzled stare followed by the comment 'What's that?' I tell them that I am really in the 'construction business' and that I partner with people to discover what they truly want in their personal lives and how to build profitable businesses.

Most people know what they do not want and often make the mistake of focusing on the 'don't wants' to the detriment of their real desires. Make no mistake, we get what we focus on, so it is up to you to focus on your true goals. With the help of a coach, you are held accountable for your actions in a non-judgemental way.

The first step is to identify a specific goal. Think of the goal as a destination and our plan to reach it as a road map. Together we devise an action-oriented strategy to achieve results much faster than you can do alone. Goals can include personal changes such as getting fit or losing weight, increasing self-confidence or improving time management skills. Business goals can be identifying your target market, attracting new clients and innovative marketing ideas.

The two most important skills that a Life Coach has are intensive listening and incisive questions. On your own when dealing with problems you 'may not see the wood for the trees'. Sometimes the coach's questions may elicit only surface answers, but with further questions the coach can get to the true issue. Sessions are conducted on the telephone which allows for full concentration on what the client is saying without any physical distractions.

As a Life Coach, I do not deal with your past – that is a therapist's job. My primary concern is where you are at the moment and where you want to go in the future. What do you want to change about the here and now? Coaches do not act as problem solvers, but serve as the catalyst for the client to find their own solutions. I will point out your strengths and not just your problem areas. Sometimes the client has the answers; sometimes the coach does. It really doesn't matter where the answers come from as long as they are found.

Now you will hear Part 2 again.
repeat Part 2
That is the end of Part 2.

Now turn to Part Three.
You will hear a radio discussion about children who invent imaginary friends. For questions 15–20, choose the answer (A, B, C or D) which fits best according to what you hear.
You now have 1 minute to look at Part 3.

Presenter: Today we're talking about children and their tendency to have imaginary friends. Liz McManus has a daughter called Caitlin, who's eight now. When she was three, she had an imaginary friend called Tytner. Liz, tell us about Caitlin and Tytner.

Mother: Well, I'll give you an example. One day I was driving Caitlin and Greg, her baby brother, home, when she solemnly informed me that Tytner was hitting the baby. So I said: 'You tell Tytner that if he does that again, he'll be walking home.' Fifteen seconds later came the inevitable news: 'He's just done it again, Mummy.' So I found myself in the embarrassing position of having to pull over, open the back door and say to this imaginary little boy. 'Tytner, out, now!' And of course, as we drove off, Caitlin started crying because her friend was standing on the pavement all alone. I had to turn back and go through the rigmarole of pulling over and opening the door to pick him up again.

Presenter: Wow, that's some story! But in fact Caitlin is no different from many children and her invented, make-believe friend is far from unusual. As many as 65% of children have had an imaginary friend at some point in their lives. The latest research suggests that invisible friends, far from being a cause for concern, should be welcomed by parents because they can help children to be more creative, confident and articulate, and have more advanced communication skills. It is thought that these findings will help reverse misconceptions about children with imaginary friends and that they will come to be seen as having an advantage, rather than

a problem that needs to be worried about. Did it worry you, Liz?

Mother: I know it does lots of parents but I never fretted about it, I think I was just amused. I'd be reading to her and I'd say, 'Is Tytner around?' and she'd say, 'Yes, he's just sitting at the end of the bed.' He became the centre of her life. She'd have tea parties with him, and he'd go to bed with her. She was shy and this was her answer. I knew she would grow out of it.

Presenter: Now Liz is one of 15 people taking part in a study of imaginary friends at the Institute of Education in London, run by Karen Majors, an education psychologist and lecturer at the institute. Karen, should parents worry about it?

Expert: Well, parents sometimes think, 'Is this healthy and how long should it go on for?' But it is a normal phenomenon for normal children. And it's very healthy.

Presenter: Why do children invent imaginary friends?

Expert: I think that children create pretend friends for many reasons: as safe, trustworthy best friends at a time when they are just starting to make real friends; as someone to confide in; and as someone to play with. Sometimes it is about wish fulfilment; children who cannot have a pet, for example, will invent one. I interviewed one little girl, aged six, who had a pony called Minty for several years. It went to school with her and the teachers knew all about it. It was a really strong relationship.

Presenter: Presumably, when they get older, children no longer have these imaginary friends. Karen?

Expert: Well, my most surprising finding is that children don't always stop having these made-up playmates when they start school. The imaginary friends often stay with them through their teenage years, providing comfort and escape – although in secret. One teenager I talked to had invented a superhero to help him through tricky patches. When things hadn't gone well at school, he would come home and play with the superhero, for whom everything always went well.

Presenter: How should parents treat these invisible people, Karen?

Expert: Well, sometimes of course parents get irritated by them – for instance, if a child insists on having the playmate at the dinner table with an imaginary setting and glass. Actually I myself had a friend called Tiger when I was young, who would sit beside me at mealtimes. But I don't think parents should tell children off for this kind of thing, or tell them that their friends are not real. Perhaps the best way is Liz's down-to-earth approach.

Presenter: How did you handle it, Liz?

Mother: Well, I patiently acknowledged Caitlin's playmate but I tried not to get involved. I never used to have to get out of the friend's way or anything. Other than that one incident in the car, Caitlin's imaginary friend didn't impinge on my life.

Expert: Yes, I agree that parents should recognize imaginary friends, but they shouldn't try to overly influence the friendship. Parents who interfere too much risk driving their children's playmates away. If they try to direct the friends, they could spoil the fantasy altogether.

Presenter: Fascinating subject, thanks for coming in to talk about it, Liz and Karen.

Now you will hear Part 3 again.
repeat Part 3
That is the end of Part 3.

Now turn to Part 4.
Part 4 consists of two tasks. You will hear five short extracts in which people are talking about the music industry. Look at Task 1. For questions 21–25, choose from the list A–H who is speaking. Now look at Task 2. For questions 26–30, choose from the list A–H the opinion each speaker expresses. While you listen you must complete both tasks.
You now have 45 seconds to look at Part 4.

Speaker 1 Yes, I choose the acts myself. People send me recordings of themselves and I give them a listen and decide whether they'd go down well here or not. We have a good crowd of regulars and I can tell pretty well what they'll like and what they won't. I think the artists who play here get a pretty good deal. Of course, this industry is full of people who are on the make, and everyone knows that artists get ripped off all the time. But I'm not like that, in fact I like to think I'm an exception to that. I try to be fair to everyone. Of course, I have to be able to keep the place going and make something for myself, but you don't have to be dodgy to do that.

Speaker 2 We get all kinds coming in here, from people who've got some chance of making it to absolute no-hopers. What I've noticed is that you get two kinds of people – the ones who are doing it out of a passion for music and the ones who are doing it because of what they think they can get out of it. Of course, I tend to prefer the former, because they're only really interested in making good music and I think that's how you should be. And it makes my job more interesting, because we can discuss what sound they're trying to create and I can help them to achieve that. I do my best for the others, too, because after all, they're paying as well.

Speaker 3 Of course, there are all sorts of stories and legends about people who do what I do, and how they left the poor artist with no money and took it all themselves. In actual fact, I've never met anyone who conforms to that stereotype. They're mostly people like me, who are in it because they enjoy it and because they want the best for their artists. I think sometimes people exaggerate our influence – sure, we can make sure our people get good contracts and the right amount of promotion, but in the end I think the ones who make it to the top would do so anyway, regardless of who's looking after them. You've either got that special something or you haven't – and if you have, one way or another, you'll make it.

Speaker 4 Yeah, we started it up years ago and it's really grown and grown. All sorts of people contribute to it and some of them have been doing it for years. Of course, the public are very fickle and things go in and out fashion very quickly. Today's big thing is soon forgotten, until people hear an old song on the radio and get nostalgic about it. But our fans are very loyal and many of them have grown up with the band. It's almost like a big family, and when the band goes on the road, they often meet people who regularly write in. And they make suggestions about things we can include in it, and I often act on those suggestions.

Speaker 5 Of course, I get to listen to all sorts of rubbish, although I always try to be fair. It frequently astonishes me that some people who really aren't any good at all make it, and some fantastically talented people remain obscure. That's the way the business works – the right manager and you're in the public eye, whether you can play or sing or not. I try to do my bit for the ones I think should make it – I give them five stars when their new record comes out, and I put in glowing comments about them. I know it has some effect – people come up to me and say that, if they hadn't seen what I said about so-and-so, they'd never have heard of them.

Now you will hear Part 4 again.
repeat Part 4
That is the end of Part 4.
That is the end of the test.

TEST 4

Part One
You will hear three different extracts. For questions 1–6, choose the answer (A, B or C) which fits best according to what you hear. There are two questions for each extract.

ONE.
You hear two people talking.

Man: Well, I suppose it had to happen some time. I mean, however good-natured you are, there's only so much bad behaviour you can take.

Woman: Yeah, I mean we've known him all these years and we've put up with all sorts of terrible scenes with him, and times when he's been awful to both of us. I'm just amazed neither of us has had the guts to say anything to him before.

Man: I'm not sure it was a lack of courage on my part. I think it was more a misplaced sense of loyalty. I mean, we go back a long way …

Woman: I know, but it's hard to come up with many good memories. Anyway, I guess it's over now and that's the last we'll see of him.

Man: Yeah, his reaction was typical. The minute we confronted him about this latest dreadful piece of behaviour, he just totally lost it. He's obviously never had any idea of the effect he has on people, even people who are supposed to be his friends.

Woman: Well, it was inevitable that it would come to this. We've said our piece, and frankly I'm glad to see the back of him. So that's that.

Man: Yeah, let's forget all about it now.

repeat extract 1

TWO.

You hear two people on the radio discussing a letter from a listener.

Man: OK, we've had a letter here from Paul, who says that his friends are into all the latest trendy hobbies and fashions, whereas he really likes trains. He's a trainspotter – he likes looking at trains and reading about them and collecting the numbers of ones he's seen – and his friends make fun of him for it. He's worried that they'll stop being his friends if he carries on with his hobby. What would you tell him, Esther?

Woman: Well, we usually end up choosing friends because we have something in common with them. Perhaps he needs to look at why he wants to be friendly with these people when they make fun of what he's interested in. I'm sure there are plenty of potential friends out there who share his interest. With them, he could enjoy that interest rather than having it used against him.

repeat extract 2

THREE.

You hear two people talking about jokes and comedy.

Woman: Well, of course, no single theory has yet been able to explain how jokes work. Even the great comedians have been stuck for a proper analysis. Of course, many jokes are written backwards with the punchline – the funny line at the end that gets the laugh – sorted out first. However, a line or a phrase doesn't necessarily need a narrative set-up to make us laugh. Witness comedy shows in which characters get laughs simply from saying catchphrases. This is also how an 'in-joke' works among a group of friends. Life itself provides the set-up, and a word or two, sometimes just a knowing look between two people who are in on the joke, provides the 'punchline'.

Man: Another thing about jokes is that a professional comedian's routine may be based on personal experience, but real experience doesn't tend to come conveniently complete with a punchline. That's why most comics are outrageous liars. It's also why some comics may even begin to provoke hilarious episodes by deliberately forgetting their wedding anniversaries or leaving their children in the supermarket.

repeat extract 3
That is the end of Part 1.

Now turn to Part 2.
You will hear a reviewer talking about a new book on the subject of children's literature. For questions 7–14, complete the sentences.
You now have 45 seconds to look at Part 2.

Woman: *Slovenly Peter*, written by Heinrich Hoffman and published in Germany in 1845, is one of the best-selling children's books ever, translated into more than 100 languages. And what a piece of work it is. A girl plays with matches and suffers horrendous burns. A boy who sucks his thumb has his thumbs cut off by the Scissor Man. The difference between that book and today's popular children's books tells us a lot about the history of children's literature. And that history is fascinatingly shown in a new book, the *Norton Anthology of Children's Literature*.

This anthology is one of the first modern, comprehensive, critical collections of children's literature. And it is intended not for children but for scholars. It shows that children's literature has now become a subject for serious academic study. The anthology, 2,471 pages long and weighing three pounds, covers 350 years of alphabet books, fairy tales, animal fables and the like, and took Jack Zipes, its general editor, and four other editors four years to compile. In it, some stories are reprinted in full, sometimes with illustrations, while others appear in the form of excerpts.

In the book, the editors trace the history of children's literature from what is probably the first children's book, *Orbis Sensualium Pictus*, an illustrated Latin grammar by Johann Amos Comenius, published in 1658. Most early children's books aimed to teach children moral lessons, and they were aimed at upper-class children, since they were more likely to be literate than other children. As today, publishers were shrewd marketers. When

John Newberry published *A Pretty Little Pocket-Book* in 1744, he included toys with the books – balls for boys, pincushions for girls.

It is striking in the anthology to see the way certain forms cross cultures. Lullabies, for instance, have a nearly universal form, with elongated vowels, long pauses and common themes of separation, hunger, bogeymen, death – as if singing of these terrors could banish them from a child's dream world.

The editors write that attitudes towards children began to change in the mid-18th century. In 1762, in his revolutionary *Emile*, Rousseau wrote that children are intrinsically innocent. In the mid to late 19th century, with the rise of the 'isms', as Mr Zipes puts it in his introduction – children were recognized as people, and their literature changed. In the late 1960s and early 1970s, as the anthology demonstrates, children's literature was approached in a different way. Nowadays, the boundaries between adult and children's fiction are disappearing. Nothing is taboo.

Now you will hear Part 2 again.
repeat Part 2
That is the end of Part 2.

Now turn to Part 3.
You will hear a radio interview with a chef about the process of eating. For questions 15–20, choose the answer (A, B, C or D) which fits best according to what you hear.
You now have 1 minute to look at Part 3.

Interviewer: I'm talking to chef Heston Blumenthal. Now, Heston, most of us think that the business of eating is pretty simple, don't we? We eat things and we like the taste of them or we don't, but you reckon it's more complicated than that, don't you?

Chef: Yes, eating is a process that involves all the senses. Any notion that food is simply about taste is misguided. Try eating a beautifully cooked piece of fish off a paper plate with a plastic knife and fork – it is not the same.

Interviewer: So how does taste operate then?

Chef: The sense of taste can be broken down into five basic categories, all of which happen in the mouth and nowhere else. These categories are: salt, sweet, sour, bitter and umami – the most recently identified taste. There is a current theory that fat is a taste but this has yet to be proved. We have up to 10,000 taste buds on the tongue and in the mouth. These regenerate, so the receptors we use today will not be the same as were used a couple of days ago. When we eat, taste buds on our tongue pick up taste but not flavour. The molecules in food that provide flavour pass up into the olfactory bulb situated between the eyes at the front of the brain. It contains hundreds of receptors that register

molecules contained in everything that we eat and smell. This is where the flavour of the food is registered.

Interviewer: OK, so our sense of smell is connected with flavour rather than taste? Is that what you're saying?

Chef: That's right. Smell and taste are registered in different parts of the head. There is a simple but effective and enjoyable way of demonstrating this. Have ready some table salt and biscuits, fruit or anything easy to eat. Squeeze your nostrils tightly enough to prevent breathing through them, but not so tight as to hurt. Take a good bite of biscuit or fruit and start chomping, making sure the nostrils remain clenched. You'll notice that it is impossible to perceive the flavour or smell of the food being eaten. Now, with nostrils still squeezed and food still in the mouth, lick some salt. Although it was impossible to detect the flavour of the food that was being eaten with clenched nostrils, the taste of the salt is unhindered. Finally, let go of your nostrils and notice the flavour of the food come rushing into your headspace.

Interviewer: I'll definitely try that some time. So what you're saying is that all the senses can affect your experience when you eat?

Chef: Yes, the brain has to process information given to it by other senses while we are eating, sometimes with surprising results. Here's another example. A few years ago at a sommelier school in France, trainee wine waiters were put through a routine wine tasting. Unknown to them, a white wine that they had just tasted had been dyed red with a non-flavoured food dye, then brought back out to taste and evaluate. Something very interesting happened. They all made notes on the assumption that the wine was what it looked like – red. In this case, the eyes totally influenced taste perception.

Interviewer: OK, so it's not just about taste, all the senses are coming into play in different ways.

Chef: Yes, and as well as allowing us to enjoy food, the senses act as warning systems, taste being the last of the sensory barriers, and bitterness the last of the taste barriers. A natural aversion to bitterness can prevent us from eating foods that could be harmful, although it appears that we have the ability to modify such basic likes and dislikes. For example, we generally grow to like bitter foods such as tea, coffee and beer as we grow older.

Interviewer: What got you interested in this business of the role played by various senses in the experience of eating? Was it just professional curiosity?

Chef: Well, I began thinking about this whole subject a couple of years ago when I noticed that more and more customers at my restaurant were commenting on the fact that the red cabbage with grain-mustard ice cream served as an appetiser just got better each time they ate it. This was the only dish on the menu whose recipe had not changed over the past year. It seemed that the barrier being presented with this dish was the vivid purple colour of the cabbage, a colour not normally associated with food. To some diners, the initial difficulty of accepting this colour interfered with the appreciation of the dish, but as they got used to it, they lost their inhibition and simply enjoyed its flavour.

Interviewer: I see. Now, of course the sense of smell must come …

Now you will hear Part 3 again.
repeat Part 3
That is the end of Part 3.

Now turn to Part 4.
Part 4 consists of two tasks. You will hear five short extracts in which people are talking about well-known people. Look at Task 1. For questions 21–25, choose from the list A–H who each speaker is talking about. Now look at Task 2. For questions 26–30, choose from the list A–H each speaker's view of the person. While you listen you must complete both tasks.
You now have 45 seconds to look at Part 4.

Speaker 1 You have to admire his achievements, how quickly he's come from nothing to being one of the most successful people in the country. As they say, the best ideas are the simple ones, and he came up with something that nobody had thought of before. And of course, as soon as he launched it, it took off. Now he's got this enormous empire and he's always on TV and in the papers. The strange thing for me, though, is that despite the fact that he must be able to run things very well, he comes across as being a bit thick. I know he can't be, but when you hear him talk, he can hardly string a coherent sentence together.

Speaker 2 Personally, I can't see what all the fuss is about. Nevertheless, lots of people obviously can, because they buy everything he produces in droves, the minute it comes out. There are even queues up the street, and when he does signings, enormous crowds gather. I don't see anything particularly original in any of it, but you have to hand it to him, he's done very well. I think it's been a case of being in the right place at the right time, rather than anything to do with quality. There are lots of people producing better things than his, but he seems to have been very fortunate and hit on something that happens to be popular right now.

Speaker 3 People laugh at him because he looks and sounds a bit funny but I think they're missing the point. He's someone who really has ideas and principles, he's not just in it to feel good about himself. And he doesn't talk all that terrible jargon, he gives a straight answer to a straight question. Not many of them do that. I get the impression that he means what he says, and that it's not just to benefit his career. I'd rather people like him were making decisions that affect all of us, not those ones who just say what they think people want to hear.

Speaker 4 People don't like him at all, because they say he's really dull and he hasn't got any real personality. But you can't expect people who do what he does to laugh and joke all the time, can you? It's all about focus – he's got it and that's why he's got so many trophies. The more interesting ones don't have the same level of consistency and aren't always in form like he is. So people tend not to notice just how good he is, and instead of giving him the praise he deserves, they go on about his personality. He's one of the all-time greats but people seldom mention that.

Speaker 5 I like what he does, and he seems to me to deal with some important issues in a way that most people don't. You have to be able to explain things that are quite complicated in a way that everyone can understand and he has a knack for doing that. The way he does interviews, for example, is very good and he always gets a lot out of the people he's talking to. And he isn't afraid to tackle things that people don't talk about much, so you learn a lot from the things he produces. I wouldn't want to argue with him, though, he's quite vicious about some of the people he deals with. It must be quite intimidating to be faced by him.

Now you will hear Part 4 again.
repeat Part 4
That is the end of Part 4.

That is the end of the test.

Paper 5: Speaking

PART 2

- What might each TV series be about?
- What might the characters be like?

- Why do these things annoy people?
- What can be done about them?

Paper 5: Speaking

PART 3

- Which aspects of tourism do these pictures show?
- Which pictures present the most positive and negative images of tourism?

Paper 5: Speaking

- What do you think the people's lives are like?
- What do you think the people's personalities are like?

- Why might the people be taking the classes?
- What might be involved in learning each skill?

Paper 5: Speaking

- What are the young people in the pictures doing?
- Which picture is most typical of young people today?

Paper 5: Speaking

- Why do you think the people are running?
- What do you think the people's lives are like?

1A

1B

1C
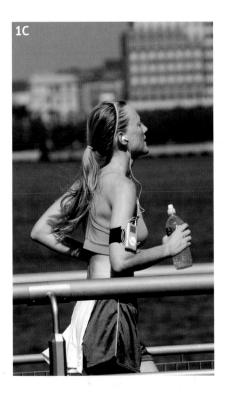

- What do you think the speakers are talking about?
- What do you think the situation is?

2A

2B

2C

Paper 5: Speaking

- Which environmental issues do the pictures show and how serious do you think each problem is?
- Which picture(s) show(s) a problem that is being solved or can most easily be solved? How is it being solved or how can it be solved?

Paper 5: Speaking

<u>PART 2</u>

- What kind of people do you think they are?
- What do you think the situation might be?

- Why do you think the people might be in these surroundings?
- What kind of people do you think they might be?

Paper 5: Speaking

- How do the pictures reflect the kind of things covered by the media nowadays?
- Which picture best reflects the influence the media has on people nowadays?